D1808291

Our Father

UNDERSTANDING GOD

Florin Marksteiner

You won't believe how simple it is

Copyright © 2015 Florin Marksteiner. All rights reserved. No portion of this book may be reproduced mechanically, electronically, or by any other means, including photocopying, without written permission of the publisher. It is illegal to copy this book, post it to a website, or distribute it by any other means without permission from the publisher.

Florin Marksteiner

10 Sherman St

Thamesville, Ontario N0P 2K0 - Canada

www.ourfatherbook.com

Limits of Liability and Disclaimer of Warranty

The author and publisher shall not be liable for your misuse of this material. This book is strictly for informational and educational purposes.

Warning – Disclaimer

The purpose of this book is to educate and entertain. The author and/or publisher do not guarantee that anyone following these techniques, suggestions, tips, ideas, or strategies will become successful. The author and/or publisher shall have neither liability nor responsibility to anyone with respect to any loss or damage caused, or alleged to be caused, directly or indirectly by the information contained in this book.

Introduction

I bet that at a certain point in your life you wondered and you wanted to understand God. You know, you had different situations and you didn't understand why it happen, you had opportunities and you missed them and you didn't understand why you missed them, you had doors that closed in your face right when you thought that the path was clear and... again you asked yourselves "Why?" not understanding the reasoning at the moment, but I bet that now, looking back, you understand and you are thankful for the way things turned out.

I promise you that by the end of this book you'll understand God as our good father. Once again: I am not a preacher, or a pastor, o a priest, or an evangelist, not even someone that can claim he has deep knowledge of the Bible, but I am someone that had an epiphany and I am really glad that I get to share.

Why I entitled the book "Our Father: Understanding God"? Is because the first two words from "Lord's Prayer" are "Our Father" and they are the most overlooked and that's happening because they are so common. Everybody rushes through the prayer and throw the first two words like the dust off a spinning tire. They zoom so fast over these two meaningful words... No one stops to really grasp how God is our father. So, this is the main reason why I'm writing the book: I want everyone to understand that God is a good father and once we all understand what a good father is, we'll all understand God. It's that simple.

I'll have plenty parables and examples that will sustain everything I say in here.

At a certain point in my life I was talking with a circle of men, it was at a men's fellowship group in a church and I don't know why it came to me to tell them that I can't wait to become a father so I can understand God. They laughed at me. They just laughed at me. And... I was hoping that, being men of church, men of faith, they would understand what I said. I was shocked to see that they were laughing at me. I opened my heart to them and they just did that. Believe it or not, I didn't go there anymore... and not because I was offended, but because they showed me that they don't understand God. Yes, the liked to fellowship, to get together and to worship God, but they didn't look like they wanted to understand Him. I think they were comfortable to just serve Him, praise Him and not get too close to Him even that they were getting together in a group with that purpose. And it's sad, because a good father always wants to embrace his children.

Time passed by and in the meantime I got to be a father and I have two beautiful girls and I can say that I totally understand God. Well, at least in some aspects. I am still living and as you know... life is an ongoing lesson. I am amazed that I understood that I will understand Him before I even became a father. I feel privileged to be able to share this with all of you. I take it as a gift that I am able to share it and pass it forward to the younger generation and especially to the boys, because I would love for the boys of today to become the good fathers of tomorrow.

Talking about good fathers, I would like to emphasize the word GOOD. Why? There are so many dads... fathers... that they are not good fathers in all the aspects of the word: the rank, the status, the privilege and the duty of being a father.

I hope that throughout the book you will understand what a good father is. I hope that even you, the ones that are growing up or

grew up without a father, you'll understand and you'll take the best and become good fathers, just like God.

So, let's get started!

Let's get to the first examples and let me show you how step by step, page by page, you will understand how being a good father you will find out how simple this life is, how simple your family life is, how simple the parenting is, how simple God's ways are and how simple everything else around you becomes once you understand that God is a good father and you're just on this Earth to mirror Him.

So guys, and girls that are reading this [get your guys to read it], it's time for you to understand God.

Dear Future Fathers

This segment is my dedication to you, my plead for you to read and enjoy the book, to get the information in and at least think of applying it. This book is for all the future fathers from around the world and when I'm saying that I am talking about you, the ones from the brink of becoming a teenager till the ones that are waiting anxiously in the delivery room to hear your first baby's cry.

If you're a teen and you are confused, let me tell you this: we all were confused at that stage and it's something normal... some of us are still confused, so don't disarm and don't panic because everything will be fine in the end. I know a lot of people tell you to just get over it or to man up. I know. The thing that they don't understand is that you are doing just that... it's just that you don't really know how, so you are trying different things. Why am I writing to you? It's because I feel that this book is especially dedicated to you. I feel that because YOU are the future of this human kind, you are the future of this society; you are the ones that will be leaders, from your families to your countries. I know that at this moment you don't see your destiny, you don't see your purpose and even a reason why you should be sticking around...

But I am telling you: **YOU HAVE A PURPOSE.**

You were born with a purpose, the most important of all. And that's not of you becoming a genius scientist or a doctor or an astronaut, no... it's to become and be a good father. We, the men, were design to lead and guide, to gain wisdom and to share it with the future generations, we were design to be fathers just like the women are designed to be mothers. Maybe you notice that I use "fathers" instead of any other words to define the role which is a duty and a privilege. That's because to be a father doesn't mean only to make a baby, to participate in the conception, but to be there all the way from the first moment you find out that you will have a child. THAT will make you a father. And from there, having the free will, you'll be able to become a good father that will be sticking around, provide, love your spouse and your future generation, your extension. The easiest way to become a good father is to mirror Our Father, God. It is the easiest way! I am telling you: read this book and let's talk in about 20 years. By that time you'll be an accomplished man and I will be an old grandpa... but I will still love to talk to you about your journey of being a father and becoming a good one.

OUR FATHER UNDERSTANDING GOD
FLORIN MARK STEINER

Razvan Nicolescu – I met him as a neighborhood teen, now a loving father and an inspiration.

A Kind of Disclaimer

Who am I to write this book?

Let me tell you who I'm not: an evangelist, a Bible thumper, an all knowledgeable in theology and doctrine, a pastor or priest. I am just a guy that had an epiphany several years ago. Such a strong one, that it stacked with me until it was impossible anymore and I had to put the word out there. And what's the best way to broadcast your thoughts but a book?

I specially didn't want to have this book edited because I want you to get to know me with my mistakes and my weird grammar, with my way of thinking and talking and to get used with my style so you can make a raw connection with me and my message.

Now, please understand: this book is firstly my own opinion and my experience and it's not meant to deviate you from your beliefs or to tell you how to live your life. This book is meant to inspire and motivate teens and adults to aspire in becoming good fathers in their future. I think it's a good cause that, if we all join in, will produce a better society all together.

That was my kind of disclaimer... now here's the official one:

- Although the author and publisher have made every effort to ensure that the information in this book was correct at press time, the author and publisher do not assume and hereby disclaim any liability to any party for any loss, damage, or disruption caused by errors or omissions, whether such errors or omissions result from negligence, accident, or any other cause.

Ok. Let's move on to more interesting parts.

I Am Grateful

Firstly, I am grateful and I thank God for pouring on me the idea of this book. It came to me in a split second and the though was simple "I can't wait to be a father so I can understand God" and it happen: I became a father and I am understanding God so deeply that sometimes I share a tear when I see what humans do to each other.

I thank God for allowing good things to happen in my life and to keep me in His favor. Each and every prayer of mine starts with "Dear God, thank you for being such a good father..." and I mean it and I love those words.

I am grateful for my family, my wife Nadine and my little girls, Ela and Dani, who shows me a lot of patience, understanding and support all the time. They, right beside God, are my rock and my support.

I am thankful to everyone that bared with me and listened to my ideas. God bless you, you're brave.

And once again: thank you God for the inspiration! I am grateful!

Our Father

who art in heaven,
hallowed be thy name.
Thy Kingdom come.
Thy will be done
on earth as it is in heaven.
Give us this day our daily bread,
and forgive us our trespasses,
as we forgive those who trespass against us,
and lead us not into temptation,
but deliver us from evil.

For thine is the kingdom,
and the power, and the glory,
for ever and ever.
Amen.

Contents

Why?

I can't wait to become a father so I can understand God.
They laughed at me.

This is a Chapter dedicated to all the "Why" questions and that's because I bet that by the time you're reading this you already asked yourself "Why?" several times.

This Chapter is about "Why men understand God better?", "Why is it so simple?", "Why mankind complicates everything?", "Why God does things the way He does?", "Why should we be obedient?", "Why should we trust?", "Why men relate to God?" and... of course "Why God is jealous?"

So all this questions have a simple answer: because He's a good father. If you read every question from above and answer with the same answer you'll see that it makes sense for all of them to have the same answer: Because he is a good father.

Now, a direct question to the men: do you see it? Do you really see it? Do you see the similarity between you and God? I'll start with the first question: "Why men relate more to God, why men understand God better?" The answer is so simple. So simple! And here it comes: it's because, by nature, they are fathers.

A woman can not be a father. And she can't be a father not because she's not a man, it's because she can not act like a father. Even if they are single moms and they take both roles to be able to provide the child or the children a good up bringing environment, they still can't be fathers. This goes the other way too. A man will not going to be able to be a mother for a child. Yes, he can try to assume the mom role, he can mirror a mom, he can carry some motherhood tasks, but will never be able to be a mom. Have you even notice a child crying for his mom and no matter what you say, what you promise, how silly you act around, until his mommy is there, he would not stop. So a woman can not be a father and a man can not be a mother. It is as simple as that.

I know that a lot of people say that God has a feminine side and yes, He does, but men relate more to God. And why? Because, even they are not fathers yet, they act like fathers. A father, a good father, please let me emphasize that. A good father lets the children evolve, lets the children learn from their own mistakes, from their own failures, lets them fall and rise again. A mom can not see her children fall, see them hurting and because of that the children become too dependent and so attached to their mother and their parents that they will not be able to make it in life at their full potential.

So that's why men relate more to God: because God has this fatherly power and strength in his heart to let us fall and rise again. And all these for our own good, for our betterment, for our growth.

Getting to the question "Why is it so simple?" makes me say that it answers by itself. It's because God made everything simple and that's because He's a good father. Every time when you want to start your children on something you give them the easiest task to do. You make it simple for them and guess what they do... exactly: they complicate it. They do it the other way, they turn it around, they don't see or they pretend they don't see how to do it right. So, that's why God made it simple for us. He wants us to grow. Like a good father, he gave us a simple world with simple rules. This leads into the answer to "Why mankind complicates everything?". It's because we are his children and because we don't understand fully at our level His ways and how things truly work, we tend to complicate things. But once we understand that His ways are simple, once we understand that we are a mirror image of Him in the way we behave, in the way we behave towards our children, in the way we teach our children, then we truly understand that is simple and we DON'T HAVE TO COMPLICATE IT.

And that's why we need to obey. That's why we need to trust God.

We want our children to trust us, right? First time when your children see you and they understand you are their father, do you think they don't trust you? Yes, they do. Did anybody told them you are their father? No... They just figured it by themselves and they trust you. By default. How come we don't trust God? Some of us didn't even trust He existed. Some of us accepted His existence and that He's our good father, but still have the shadow of doubt in their hearts. How good it is to trust your father, to trust in who he is and that what he does if for your good. As I said, a good father makes it simple for his children to understand the things surrounding them, the environment and eventually the life and the world. That's where we have to trust in Him in doing the simple things in life how He designed us to do them. And I am talking here about anything. Simple things like relationships: with your spouse, with your children, with your co-workers. There are so many situations that have simple solutions, but we choose the hard way, the drama, the complicated way and that's because we don't trust our father's ways, the simple ones.

Going back to the moments where children acknowledge that we are their fathers I have to say that those are the moments when we become their fathers. Yes, biologically, we became their fathers nine months before they were born, spiritual, psychological and in all the other aspects, we become their fathers as long as they acknowledge that we are their fathers because until that moment, we are just people with children. As soon as they know that we are "dada" we are their fathers. And being good fathers, we embrace them, we love them and we want the best for them and every time we want to do that we want to do it the simple way so they can get it, so it's easy for them to understand that we love them.

In this book there going to be a lot of examples from my own personal life in relation to my children because I don't want anyone to think that I'm stealing their personal life. Ha!

So, getting to the last question: "Why is God jealous?" I'll answer with a simple example that I will tell you about in the next chapter...

Jealousy

Do you think God's right to be jealous sometimes?
It's an open question.
Me, personal... I think I answered it.

We maybe heard from people or maybe read it in the Bible that God is a jealous God and of course some of us were or still thinking that that's not a good thing. Now, the big question is: "Why God is jealous?" I'll tell you a little parable so you understand why God is jealous and why his jealousy is good.

Every time when somebody comes to our place and our little daughter, about three years old at the time, she would talk to the person and she would get a candy or a present from them, she will just, by default, love them because this is what a three year old knows, what translates into affection for her. So, I would get to the point where someone would bring her a present every time he or she would come over and after they left I would go to hug my daughter and she would just ask me about that person over and over again. That would make me jealous. Here I am trying to have a moment with my daughter and in the middle of it, she would just focus her attention on the person that brings presents. It wasn't a bad jealousy, but it would be jealousy... I was thinking: "here I am, I am hugging you, I love you, I want to show you my love, I am here for you every day and you're asking me about that person?"

This kind of jealousy is what God has for us, His children. Not the kind where He's chasing you down with an AK47 and wants to end your life because He suspected you love someone else. It's a good kind jealousy. Why I'm saying this is because you, as a good father, you want to give the best to your children and you're doing your best to provide for them, to give them everything you can, of course with some limits, and to be there for them as much as you can to make sure they have a good upbringing and that they are getting the best of you.

Now, when your child gets swiped with some little presents and candies, things that you don't do on the daily bases because it's not healthy for their development, and doesn't stop talking about

the person that brings the treats, you feel the jealousy taking more territory in your heart.

We are deterred all the time by some little present and gifts that keep our eyes and our heart off God. He gives us the best He can give us, which is the best of the best, because he's a good father. But again, we are swiped away by little temptations, little things that other people and even other entities give to us... and that makes Him jealous. Let me ask you: Isn't that a normal thing? Did you ever have that kind of jealousy as a father in any stage of your children's development? I bet you did...

For those that you don't have children: did you ever think of some episodes in your life when you were a child that maybe your father had that kind of moment when he maybe felt jealous because maybe some of his friends were playing with you more than him and that's not because he didn't want to play with you but maybe he didn't have to opportunity to do it because of work. Or maybe he didn't have the money to buy you a certain bicycle and a friend saw the need, and being kind, brought one over with a bow on it and your father felt jealous because he wanted to be able to do that, to fill that role and be able to produce that excitement for you.

So, what do you think? Do you think God's right to be jealous sometimes? It's an open question. Me, personal... I think I answered it.

3

Love Is

...NOT JUST HUGS AND KISSES...

...not just hugs and kisses. Yes, love is beautiful. In general it means to be gentle towards people, it means to keep the peace and to want the best for the others.

But the father love is a little bit different. A father shows love not just by hugging and kissing his children, by playing and spending time with them, by giving them toys and games, but by teaching them to discern good from evil, by teaching them and sharing his experience and wisdom, by discipline them and doing everything in his power to guide his children and help them on the long run to become good parents at their time.

A lot of times, especially in the modern society, if you want to discipline your child, is categorized as abuse. No, I tell you: that's love, fatherly love. Now, we need to make a clear difference in between disciplining and beating up a child. Disciplining a child happens when the child did something wrong, did something that doesn't stand with the family and the house rules, with the core values that the child is raised in. The discipline comes as a consequence of his or her actions. Think of the last time you got a speeding ticket. That was disciplining. There are ways and ways to discipline a child and we'll not elaborate them here, but the main purpose of the discipline is to make the child understand that what he or she did was wrong and that it shouldn't happen again. Sounds familiar? Getting back to the speeding ticket... what does that Police Officer tells you before you're free to go? "Slow down" which means "or I'll ticket you again". So that's the discipline and it can manifest from a simple look to a talk to a "time out" to an ear being pulled or even, the worst case scenario, a "spanking". And remember: it's all in love as the Proverbs 13:24 says: "Whoever spares the rod hates their children, but the one who loves their children is careful to discipline them." And why? Because without the discipline, the children have no guidance, they are not steered towards the good path, channeled to grow in good spirit and choosing the good at all times. A child with no

discipline will always jump from side to side not knowing what to choose in life and because of that will end up in places that didn't want to be in the first place and neither did the parents.

So that was the discipline which is an important part of the fatherly love. As I said, let's differentiate the discipline from abuse. We've seen that discipline comes when we, as parents, want to correct and guide our children, with love, to steer them away from the wrongs they do. The abuse, on the other hand and in my opinion, is totally the opposite. The abuse comes upon the child with no fault, comes with anger and from external issues, comes in unimaginable forms from people that you can hardly call them parents. If you ever had that in your life as a child remember: it wasn't your fault and you don't have to retaliate against anyone. You were just the easy target that they could pour their anger on to go on with their lives. I know that if you had these kind of episodes in your life it hurt a lot, not so much physical but in your heart and in your spirit wondering all the time what did you do wrong and why is that you are the one that gets it all the time. I know that at the time you were torn, confused and lost, with dark thoughts and nothing to cling to and most of all not feeling loved. Do you still feel like that? Is it still happening to you? If it does, then let me tell you that you have the power to stop it, you are entitled to contact agencies and other organizations that will be able to change the situation for you. The only thing you need to do is to take the decision to make it stop, to call someone you trust and tell them everything that's happening so you can be set free. If it stopped sometime in your past, let me tell you that it's good to let the past be history, to forgive and forget, to move on and promise yourself that you'll never do something like that to anyone, especially your children. I managed a retirement home at a point in my life and I got to learn why some of the residents never had visitors: not because it was way out of the way for the children to visit, but because they

abused their children that now, when they were old and they would love to have someone to visit them, the children had not enough love for them to be motivated to even think of visiting.

Tell me: is it worth to spill your anger on your children? Definitely not. God gave us the miracle of having children so we can cherish and love the little ones because time flies and they will return that love later on: unconditional love. I am begging you, no matter at what stage are you right now in this life, if you're a teen, a married man, a father: love your children with the fatherly love, with godly love, love them in all the ways you can and show them your love. It's for your own good. It's what God does to you unconditionally, to all of us, His Children.

4

Trust

A GOOD FATHER INSPIRES TRUST IN HIS CHILDREN.

Let's talk about trust a little bit.

I know it sounds weird if I ask you, but... do you trust your father? Do you trust him, not just because he is your father, but do you trust him as a person, because of what he does for you, do you trust his actions, do you trust his thoughts, do you trust his intentions for you?

I am asking this because us, as human beings, are programmed to trust our parents from the first moments we arrive in this world, but as you look around, there are a lot of children today that get mistreated by their parents and that leads them to not trusting them, to not loving them, not wanting to be with them but to be far away from them and anyone else.

So, you see... it's not enough to be just a father but to be a good father and a good father inspires trust in his children. Whenever a good father embraces his children, his children feel peace, love, kindness and they feel secure, that they are protected and their father is there for them no matter what.

Just a little example to show you what it means to inspire trust: We were at the pool with our first born Ela and she was only three at the time. We played around the pool, we had fun with the diving toys, we ran around and so on. I'll admit it... I'm a little kid when it comes to play around water... While we were doing that, a though came into my mind: "what if I test Ela's trust in me?" I know... some of you think that's too early to do that. But, I took her in the water with me, we played, we splashed, we had fun together and then I raised her up on the edge of the pool and I moved back saying "Ok. Jump in the water. I am here to catch you" and I stretched my arms towards her so she can see that I will keep my word. I was a little bit hesitating in my mind because I thought that she will not jump because she won't trust me... but I didn't have time for that doubting thought because she didn't even blink, she went for it: ran all the way to the edge and jumped. Remember: she was only three. She didn't doubt me. I was really glad to know that she's trusting me. It made me feel like I am a good father and I am doing a good work being a good father, it gave me the confirmation that I needed and motivated me more to work on improving and being even a better one.

It is good to feel trusted. It makes you feel good as a person. Wherever you are, in your family, in society, if you know people trust you, it makes you feel good because that gives you authority and builds your personality, your character by giving you confidence and confirmation that you're a good person. We all want to be good people. We were designed to be good.

This is how God feels when you trust Him... When you have the FAITH to trust him to fall into His arms all the time, in good times, in bad times, if you learn to just jump into His arms and let him catch you because you trust Him, then your relationship with Him builds and deepens even more. You already know that every relationship in this world is based on trust and when you have full trust in someone, with no doubts, then you have faith in that person. See how simple it is?

As you see, it's all based on trust and on faith. Why I say faith? Because when you see first time your father... how do you know he's your father? You never seen him in your life... but you know he's your father especially if your mom, the person that you grew in and grew with, tells you he's your father... you trust him, and you trust him especially if he's nice with you, if he smiles kindly to you, if he caresses you nicely, if he gives you a sense of love and security, you trust him fully no matter what, you have faith in him. He's your daddy. Period.

By default, God is our father and if we learn to be children and to trust him, we become good fathers because we'll mirror Him, and we'll end up doing everything He does and act how He acts. If you don't believe me, go the easy way: ask your pastor or someone that you know they know the Bible to give you some examples on how God acted like a father. I am sure they will supply you with a bunch of examples. Now, I would encourage you to read the Bible, but I think it's easier and a little bit better to ease yourself in by asking someone than to just dive into it and not knowing what to read and where to start. In some of the chapters you found some similarities in between our behaviour and God's actions. Some of you might not agree... but it is that way because as soon as you become a father you'll start acting like God: you will teach your children, discipline them, lead them, love them, help them, not help them when you know they can manage themselves, your behaviour will change into a fatherhood series of actions and feelings... and guess what? All these are all Godly. How do you feel now, if you're a father? How do you think you'll feel when you'll become a father, a good one?

If you're a father right now, try to give your children the opportunity to trust you in any situations, unconditionally. If you're not a father yet, build your personality so you can inspire trust in everyone around you, in your spouse and eventually in your children.

That's really important.

5

You Can Do It!

IF I WOULD'VE CUT THAT ACTION BEFORE
SHE WOULD EVEN THINK THAT SHE'S CAPABLE OF DOING IT.
OF CLIMBING THE STAIRS AND THEN GO DOWN THE SLIDE BY HERSELF.
I WOULD'VE JUST BEEN A BAD FATHER.

Let's jump to the other side of the spectrum, the other side of the story where, in this society, doing something for your children or teaching your children something in a certain way you look like a bad dad and I'll explain you how.

Maybe you've seen the title "You can do it"...

A lot of times our children, because they don't know their strength, they don't know their capacity, they are afraid of doing a lot of things because they don't know they can do them. But us, as good fathers and as good parents, we know that they have the potential to accomplish different things. And because of that, it's not bad to push them a little bit, to explain to them that they are prepared and they can do it. Pushing them is a way to enhance the child development. Encouraging them to do different activities that they don't trust themselves, and their capabilities, is good parenting (in the limits that you know that your children are capable).

Simple example: I bet it happen to you too... when you were a child or just now when you became a father. Ok. Me and my daughter at the playground. She's two. She runs from my side and, alone, climbs the stairs up to reach on the top of the slide, she sits to prepare to go down the slide and stops there waiting for my reaction. I am looking at her and, being the first time she did that, as a good father I had fear in my heart because I don't want my children to get hurt. But... In my brain, in my mind and in my spirit I know she can do it. What did I do? I just told her: " Yeah, sure. Go on. You can do it. Daddy's here."

"Daddy's here"... It sounds so good and so familiar. I love it. It's such a warm feeling when you, as a child receive those words. It's just like your daddy just put a nice warm blanket on you, gave you a hot chocolate and snuggled you, just like you'd be ready to watch a movie. How beautiful it sounds "Daddy's here... Daddy's

here." I know that every time when I say that, God says that to me... and to us.

So, what does she do? She smiles, she looks at me and let go. And she went down on that long slide and I watched her with pride every inch of that slope and at the end of the slide, who do you think caught her? Exactly! Me. I was there in a second and I lifted her in the air with a big proud smile on my face. What do you think she did as soon as she escaped my arms? She went straight back on the top of the slide and went down without stopping because she knew that daddy is there to catch her.

If I would've gone to grab her, to tell her "No, no! Don't go there! You might hurt yourself. You can't do this. You are not big enough." If I would've cut that action before she would even think that she's capable of doing it, of climbing the stairs and then go down the slide by herself, I would've just been a bad father. I knew that she is capable. Her actions showed me that she knew that too. So, why should I stop her in the path of gaining courage and confidence, of accomplishing something, of learning? Just because I had a grain of fear in my heart? That's selfish and a good father is not.

"You can do it!"

We are told that all the time in circumstances that we think we can't overcome, in situations that we think are the worst and we are lost. But we are told over and over again that we can do it by OUR father, by God. How many times you seen in the Bible so many people asking God "Why me? Why did you choose me? I am just an ordinary man. I can't do this." and God, our father, our good father tells them that they can. God never said something like "I'll take a second chance on another guy" or "Yeah, you're right. You're not good enough." No. He says "You can do it!"

19

Is that simple! Take all this and reflect it into yourself and into your children and you'll be amazed how good it is and how good it feels to be a good father and to feel like God. And I am not saying to feel like you are a God, but to feel like how He feels... and you'll understand.

6

Surprise!

THE BEST WAY TO GIVE A PRESENT TO A CHILD
IS TO MAKE IT INTO A BIG SURPRISE.

Ok. Let me ask you something: What's the best way to give a present to a child? Come on, think a little bit. Think of what was the best way you got a gift when you were a child. Think how it felt, think how you expressed your excitement and then think how would've you reacted if the gift was just handed to you. So, what was the best way? Exactly! Surprise them!

The best way to give a present to a child is to make it into a big surprise and to deliver when it's least expect it. Why? Because the excitement goes through the roof and that is your biggest reward. Why would you surprise the child and not just hand the present to them in a bland way? Because it's boring! And children don't like boring... as we all know. Did that happen to you any time? Did your parents surprise you with a present you didn't expect? How did you feel in those moments? How do you think they felt? Let me tell you that nothing makes parents feel better than seeing their children happy. Nothing. Parents: am I right? Well, in the same way, God, being our good father loves to surprise us whenever He has the chance. Whenever you have a desire, like in other chapter of the book, He already knows it and he's preparing to craft a plan to have you surprised. The beautiful thing is that every time when he surprises us, he gives us a lot more than we wanted, He's blessing us with a lot more than our desire because He loves to see us happy.

So, if you're growing to be men, to be fathers, I advise you to not forget to surprise your children with the things that they like, with the things that you think they are right for them and they like them. It will make them happy, but, man it will melt your heart seeing them so happy. And if that happens to you, remember in those moments to pat yourself on the back because you are there, you are a good father that mirrors God and that will raise his children, and especially his boys to become a mirror of God, to became good fathers.

7

Love All

So, THAT'S WHAT A GOOD FATHER DOES:
LOVE ALL HIS CHILDREN, WITH NO FAVORITES,
WITH THE SAME STRENGTH,
BUT IN DIFFERENT WAYS.

Let's talk about a father's love towards his children.

I am talking now to fathers that have more than one child. For those who are not fathers yet... listen to this.

You have the first child and you gave everything you were able to give because it was the first time when you became a father and it was a new experience, it was the new you that you needed to discover and embrace as your life long role. Then... it came the second... the third... the forth... and, you never know... earlier in the days it was ten.. eleven... twelve. So, what a father supposed to do with his love for his children in these cases? Did the love run out? Did it just faded out at the second or third child? No. A good father loves ALL his children with the same strength, giving them all the same kind of attention and making them feel loved. And of course... he has no favourites. When I'm saying he has no favourites it means that he doesn't show more love to one particular child ignoring the other ones. Why am I saying that? Maybe you've seen that a lot of times children are jealous. You give an apple to one, the other one wants an apple too... and they start crying and they might even get at each other because of the feeling. It's good to give an apple to each child. That shows that you're sharing the love and each of them receive the same ratio of love, but we have to remember that all of them are different, all the children need to be loved in their unique ways. If you explain that to your children, they will understand to not be jealous on each other and they will understand that everyone needs love in a different way. Did you know that there are five major kinds of love? The parenthood embraces three types: storgy, agape and philos.

Storgy - is the love one has for a dependent. It is commonly called "motherly love." It is one of the stronger loves, because it involves a commitment that relies on only one trait of the receiver – that he or she is dependent.

Agape - is the love, in its purest form, that requires no payment or favour in response. The most common word for God's love for us is Agape.

Philos - is the love that signifies spontaneous natural affection, with more feeling than reason.

To become a good father remember to not favour children, but to love them in equal quantities and in different ways, in ways that they feel and need love. Don't worry... you will find out what each of your children need to feel loved. The easiest way to find it out is to pay attention when they are babies. All the newborns have the basic needs but they have their own specific needs while they develop their character. If you pay attention to that and cater to their affection needs, you'll learn fast how each of them need to get love from you and how you have to deliver. It's pretty easy and believe me: you have it in you, so don't be afraid. It's like when you want to hold a newborn in your arms for the first time and you're afraid you'll drop the baby or you're not holding proper and so on, but once that little bundle got in your arms, your primary instincts kick in and you just know it.

Even that there will be some jealousy from the other children, they have to understand that you love them all but in different ways and not because you want to, but because they need it. So, that's what a good father does: love his children, all his children, with no favourites, with the same strength, but in different ways.

Now, would you agree that we are all different in this world, that we are all unique and we all need love, we need to be loved? Well, we need different kinds of love and the beautiful thing is that God gives us all His love and He gives us exactly what we need. We just need to open our heart and to receive that love. We have to open our mind and to understand that God IS Love!

He shares His universal love with each one of us. Never say that God doesn't love you because He's a good father and he loves you a lot and unconditionally. Never say you're favoured because is not true. Christian or not, God loved everyone with the same strength, but He loves us different. So, make sure you tell God how you like to be loved, what makes you feel loved. It's exactly how your children, when they were babies, let you know when they were comfortable and secure in your arms and they felt loved and you knew what to do next time and how to love them... and maybe you noticed that, growing up, they kept the same kind of love close to their hearts and maybe they added another one.

What kind of love do you need?

 God has it and he gives His love to you every day, you just have to open your heart and your mind, take a step back and recognize with gratitude that is happening... every single day.

8

Universal Love

WHEN YOU HAVE MORE THAN ONE CHILD
YOU WANT THEM TO GROW
TOGETHER AND BE FRIENDS

We all know people that have children while we're still young and we're not married and when we get to see them first time, how do we feel? We change our stance, our posture, our spirit, we brighten up and we even put a funny persona welcoming the little one in our lives. We almost become fathers in that moments, over and over again. Why do I say that? It's because it is a feeling close to the one that you have when you get to see and hold your first child, your very own, the one that will call you dad for the rest of your life.

I know there is no strong connection when you are in a situation like that, but that universal love kicks in and you change in a second. There are some people that try to resist and fake the fact that they are not impressed how much they care about a little human being like that or they pull back being afraid that their true self will come out in the light and everyone will see them for who they really are: men that like to nurture and protect any child, theirs or not.

I grew up in a communist society and even that a lot of people said it was bad, and it was in some aspects, I had something that a big part of the world wish they had: community parenting . Yes, in that type of society everyone was looking after each other, and their children. I remember having neighbours pointing out to me if I did something wrong or even disciplining me for that, I had my friends' parents taking me and showing me different talents and traits, guiding me in resolving some problems, I had people from the neighbourhood mentioning and complimenting me for my good manners. All that beside my parent's love, education, discipline and guidance. You know that saying, right? "It takes a village to raise a child"... well it does. It does because us as children, we need to learn, to absorb as much information, good information, as we can and we need to become social... and the best way to do that is to be out "in the village" to interact with the people we know because doing that we test our good manners,

our intelligence, our skills and we benefit of the most important thing: the universal love that they will surround us with.

Once I grew up, it was my turn to show the love and it came all natural. Every time when I've got in contact with babies and toddlers, I instantly became a clown and I flew down to their level, physically and mentally, and connected with the little ones. It took a while for me to recognize that this is how universal love manifests. You know that feeling: you smile without control, your eyes are brighter, you want to be funny for no reason, you just want to draw a smile on their face or even yank a giggle from them. And when I say them, I am not talking just about children. Your universal love can manifest toward anyone, yes, towards any person. Now, in this society, where everything is sexualized, any sight, gesture or word has a sexual connotation and a bad misuse, it is harder to manifest your universal love. A nice compliment, a smile and a touch, a friendly hug... all these are now in the "hitting" arsenal. With the "rainbow" and "pride" movements, it's hard to share your love with another man by giving him a sincere heart felt hug because now every man feels embarrassed if he's being hugged, feels awkward and, sadly... a lot of people lost the notion of sharing their love, the true universal one, with everyone. I've witness in church men hugging "brotherly" and there's so much awkwardness and blushing and side hugs with shoulders in the other's chest, and fist bumps and distant air hugs, and manly back slaps, but nothing sincere and raw. I was telling some people: "hug me now because if I die tomorrow, you'll be sorry" and they were laughing... but they didn't know how much truth is in that. And I think it's sad that people would give up the raw, embedded love that we have in us since we're stepping into this world because a group of people are acting different and are stealing the joy of sharing the true love. Another times I would tell people "you don't want to give me a hug now, but if right now it would be a war and you've been stranded and hungry and thirsty

and depressed and you got to see me, you would've run to hug me." I tell them that to make them understand how they take this so light and how they don't give it a chance.

God design us to "love one other" and when He did that, He meant it in the most pure way. Why did He do that? Because He wants all His children to get along, to coexist and to thrive together. When you have more than one child you want them to grow together and to be friends, you want then to love and respect each other, to cherish their siblings and to have a harmonious relationship. How do you feel when you see them yelling at each other or even getting in a physical fight? Exactly... you don't like it. You want the best for them and that starts from them feeling for each other that universal love that we, as good fathers, inspire in them.

9

Ask And You Shall Receive

IT'S SO SIMPLE AND AMAZING.
JUST CAREFUL ON HOW YOU ASK
AND WHAT YOU ASK FOR.

I can say that was one of the first things that I learn from the Bible.

Growing up, I wasn't religious and I wasn't going to church even that I was having deep roots in a religion ruled orthodox society. In that kind of society, if you'd want to ask God something you'd need to go talk to the priests and they would be the interface in between you and God... and a lot of the priests weren't saints, if you know what I mean.

But with time, when I wanted something really bad, I was thinking or voicing out "I would love to have that" or "I would love to do that" and I realized that our children do the same thing. First they ask us "I want that!". At least at the beginning, this is how they ask and I am sure this is how we asked too.

With time we all grew to learn that if we ask nice and if we're polite and ask in a certain way including the magic words, we'd get almost anything. Then, there is the other way of asking for things and that's showing the desire. When your children tell you "I would love to have that" or "I would love to do that" your heart melts and you burn to get it for them. It might not be in ten minutes, one hour, one day or one week, but you'll get it for them because you know they want it from the deepest depths of their heart.

Ask and you shall receive. It's so simple and amazing. Just careful on how you ask and what you ask for.

10

Patience

WE ARE ANXIOUS OR AFRAID.
BUT WE WOULD LOVE TO SEE
THAT PROPHECY COMING THROUGH.

You know what Jesus said when He left this Earth?

He said:

"I am going away and I am coming back to you." [John 7:33] and from what the entire Christian world knows, Jesus is God because he admit it saying: "I am" and he proved that He is and when He left the Earth He said He will be back. We all know that everyone is waiting for the second coming, that everyone would love to see Jesus and God, to be right there in front of them.

But when is He going to be back?

It sound so complicated, but it's so simple.

For us it's hard to understand it. Remember, we are his children. We are anxious or afraid, but we would love to see that prophecy coming through.

Let me show you how simple it is: Let's say I'm waking up in the morning and preparing to go to work, my little toddler daughters are seeing me, we have breakfast together and they see me leaving, but before I leave, seeing their sad faces, I would tell them: "I'll be back home. I'll be home by five o'clock." and leave. They are still sad, but I know that in about five minutes they will find something to play with and forget about being sad. Now, they are toddlers and they don't know the notion of time and measuring time so they don't know what it means "five o'clock". After a while they are wondering where daddy is and they start waiting for him to come home. And they are waiting and waiting and waiting... and he's still not opening that door. They know that daddy said he will be back, but when? And they don't know. They are just waiting there. They start to lose their patience, they start asking mommy, mommy reassures them that daddy will be home soon, that they don't have to worry because daddy will be home.

The girls would ask "When daddy home?" and mommy would say "at five o'clock"... ok... When is five o'clock? They don't know. They don't understand that notion yet.

So, they are playing, watching TV, they are doing anything they can to keep themselves busy until the time comes when daddy should be home. But still... it starts to get really late. For them, not for me. They lose their patience, their peace, they don't know what's happening and they might even panic, they are afraid that daddy is not going to come any more. But! At a certain moment the door opens and daddy's home! It's five o'clock. He's home just as he promised.

Now, if they are smart children, they would see the sign when daddy is coming home and what would be the normal signs? You hear a car engine, you might see some lights and reflections on the walls thought the window, you hear some steps on the porch and you might hear the keys in the door.

If you think a little bit, Jesus said the same thing: "These are the signs you'll know I'm coming" and described in the Bible the series of signs that we should look for before His coming. Why did He do that? Because we can't grasp God's notion of time. We know our time, because, if you remember, we invented the time measurement. Us, the people. So, to be able to understand God, we need to be able to simplify everything and to understand that God's timing it's His timing, not our timing.

It's so simple: you as a dad telling your children you're leaving and that they will see some signs when you're coming home. Guess what? They will be waiting for you in front of the door with a big smile on their faces because they know you're coming home. Am I right? Yes, I am.

Obedience

IF YOU'D LISTEN OBEDIENT.
WITHOUT QUESTIONING.
WITH FAITH.
YOUR LIFE WOULD'VE BEEN A LOT EASIER

This is the toughest subject when it comes to Faith and when it comes to God. Why?

I bet you face some situations or some stages when your children are not too obedient... Or, if you remember and if you're honest to yourself, you will remember when you weren't obedient towards your parents.

Well, let me explain to you why we need to be obedient.

So, you tell your children to do something, something really simple, let's say to tie their shoes and they don't want to do it. Why? Too busy running around, don't want to stop from playing or just plain and simple don't want to listen to you... But they don't understand why you tell them to do that. And I am not stopping just at shoelaces, I am referring here to all the situations where you tell them to so something and they don't understand, in that moment, why they should do it. The thing is that when you're telling them that they need to do something, you know all the reasons why and in the shoelaces case if they don't tie them they might trip and fall and hurt themselves. So, that's why you tell them to do it. To prevent something that you know it will happen if they don't take the proper action. But them, in that moments, not understanding your reasoning and that's because they don't look ahead and they can't understand your angle and your point of view, they go on without tying their shoes. Guess what? Who do you think is coming to you with their knees scraped and bleeding, tears in their eyes, dirty hands and ripped pants as they just tripped and fell because of their own shoelaces? Exactly...

Now, picture you being the one that doesn't want to tie his shoelaces...

Have you been in this position before? You know... when God tries to tell you to do something and you keep doing your thing and you ended up getting hurt? If you'd listen obedient, without questioning, with faith, without trying to do it your way, your life would've been a lot easier. It's never too late to start doing that. Isn't that simple?

It's so simple that it should make you want to be obedient all the time.

And you, as a good father, should teach your children to be obedient. God gave a major rule to people regarding that: "Honour your mother and father" and to honour parents means to be obedient to them. Did you ever think that being obedient to God, you honour Him? See how simple it is? Think about it.

Promises

YOU DELIVER YOUR PROMISES IN YOUR TIMING,
LIKE A GOOD FATHER THAT YOU ARE.

What's happening when you're promising your children something?

First of all, they are expecting for you to deliver, to deliver fast. And... they are excited. For you, you love their excitement, their expectation and build up till the moment when you deliver what you promised.

Now, we know it's easy and simple when you make small promises, but what's happening when you make big promises?

Let's see... Let's say you promise your son or daughter that when they will be sixteen you'll get them a car. At the present moment you don't know yet how you'll do it, but you have the strong desire to get them the car and bring a happy feeling in them, you fill up with their excited expectation that builds up day by day and year by year. In the meantime, you craft a plan to make the ways in buying the car. Everything works by the plan.

The day is coming and the moment is there. You pull out the keys and you see the excitement reaching its peak and exploding into a big uncontrollable smile, a laugh that turns into cry and in laugh again, in endless hugs and in jumping and skipping around.

How do you feel in that moment? Who do you think is happier in that moment? YOU!

They might be able to express it in a more effervescent way but your happiness is way stronger knowing that you were able to

keep your promise. And... you want to keep your promises because this is what a good father does, what God does.

Switching to the relationship between you and God, sometimes you feel like God is not keeping His promises... but a lot of times we forget that everything is happening in His timing. Let me paint that for you: once you promised your son or daughter the car, because of the excitement, they start noticing the makes, the models, the dealerships and even deals that eventually they point out to you: "this one would be nice" hoping that maybe that one will be the one and that this one will be the day. But you know that, first of all, it's not the day that was in the promise and then, that you want to give them the best and you'll look for a car that meets your criteria of safety, economy, price, reputation, style and so on. They might have a say in the color picking and... maybe gadgets. But the timing and the last word is yours.

We need to understand that. Once we do, we'll know to respect God's promises and NEVER doubt Him. That's FAITH.

Ok. Let me turn it around. Let's say that right before you want to purchase the car a situation arises... Let's say you have a death in the family. Someone close. Someone so close that you have to change plans and priorities and shift the funds towards the funeral. I think that can happen to anyone. Am I right? Am I reasonable? Ok.

That would put a hold on your promise. What are the feelings in this moment? Your child is for sure disappointed, you're feeling

guilty even it's not your fault, your close ones feel like you didn't deliver...

But! If you are and been a good father, your family knows to assess and respect the situation, to be understanding and to trust in you that you will deliver and that now is not the right time, but you will deliver.

We already know that you want to keep your promise. We already know that God, the one that we mirror, keeps His promises. Just look retrospective in your life and notice the promises he delivered already, maybe not in your right time, but for sure in His. And: the promises you think he didn't keep... just put yourself into the expectation stance and rejoice knowing that they will be delivered.

Remember: God's a good father... and a good father ALWAYS keeps his promises. Do you? If not, it's not too late! You deliver your promises in your timing, like a good father that you are.

13

Help Offer

HOW DO YOU THINK GOD PULLS BACK, LETTING US STRUGGLE IN OUR OWN STUBBORNNESS?

So, years go by and now my little girl, because we have two children now, she's the big one... even that she's still small. Let me set the stage:

Her fourth birthday: The grandparents are buying her a push scooter with princesses all over the frame, nice wheels, gorgeous little toy that... came in a box and it needs to be assembled. Of course, daddy as a good father, tells the little girl "I'll help you to put it together" at which she replies with a tiny proud voice "No. I'll do it by myself"

Now, going back a few chapters, I AM the guy that says "You can do it!" but in this moment it wasn't the case because it needed to follow a diagram, there were bolts and nuts, tools and a bunch of little things that made the gift into a puzzle. I asked her again "Are you sure?" and she replied with the same pride "Yes!" so I stepped back. I accepted her wish. At that moment I felt so useless and so disappointed that she doesn't trust me enough to let me help her. I can say I was feeling anger. Not towards her, but towards her decision. I just wanted to help. Nothing else. So, I let her try it... And I should've taken some pictures because that scooter wasn't coming along the way it was designed to be. It was anything else but a scooter. So much that if I wanted to ever start my girl in abstract sculpture, that was it, that was the moment. Several minutes go by, my feelings are back to normal and even better because of the show she was putting on trying to put it together. The funniest part was that suddenly she says "Ok I'm done!" and I am looking at her, she looks at me and I ask her "Does it look like the one on the box?" and of course she tells me "NO..." and I asked her "So, how come you're done?" and she kept telling me that she's done. What she was telling me in fact was that she was done trying not that she finished to put the scooter together. I felt like this was a right moment to ask again "Would you like me to help you?" I need to underline the question here: "Would you like me to help you?" I didn't asked

her to do it instead of her, but help her to assemble it together and mostly for me to guide her and hand her parts so she can put the hands on the tools and parts and learn to understand how things fit together. And guess what she tells me? "No, I can do it all by myself!" Again... Proud. And I let her be...

Two minutes later? She was done again. So then I had to be a good father, step in and tell her "Listen honey, I'll do it for you." and I did it and of course she was happy because she got to try it to go outside and roll it in the neighbourhood.

Now tell me something: how do you think God feels when every time, with very problem we have, we are offered the help, the solution, which usually is a simple solution and we turn Him down? Why do you offer to help someone? Because you love them. I know, not that kind of love, but the universal one, the one that makes us all connect. God loves us and all the time He offers us the easiest way out of situations and conflict it's just that we love to complicate things and we want to do everything by ourselves, with no help.

How do you think God pulls back, letting us struggle in our own stubbornness, watching us from the corner and smiling knowing that any moment you'll give up and ask for help? Here I'm talking with the fathers: how do you feel when you see your child fail and you know he or she can do better if your help would be accepted? You feel disappointed, you feel anger, you want to be useful, for them to accept your help, to reap the joy of doing things together faster and easier and just enjoy the experience and the moment.

Let me tell you: in this kind of moment, God is sad. And He's sad because He knows that through Him us, as His children, can go through life in an easier way. Exactly how us, as fathers, we want our children to not face huge challenges and their lives will be

smooth and pleasant, that they will be successful and achieve their full potential.

So, it's good the let our father help us and it's good the recognize the moments when He wants to help us, it's just not good to let Him do all the work...

1
4

More Patience

PATIENCE IS THE ELEMENT THAT KEEPS YOU SANE.

I know… we're talking about patience. Now, I have to tell you that Patience is the biggest virtue a parent, and especially a father, has. In this times and this society where everything happens and has to happen almost instantly and the present is "so yesterday", we need to learn to be patient, to take a step back, take a breath and think of decisions, learn to listen, learn to let the circumstances lead us to where we need to be. The hardest part is to really let ourselves be guided… and that takes time and patience to learn. Why should we learn to be patient? Why do we need it? Why is so important?

Patience is the element that keeps you, the man, the head of the family, the one that gears and steers the family towards goals, towards a better life and towards harmony, sane. Remember how many times you just reacted to something, how many times you just spring into action like a resort without thinking and regretted later because you didn't understand the moment's circumstances, or how people say, the big picture? And all that because you didn't take the time to understand what's happening or you weren't able to understand because the entire situation was beyond your understanding as a human.

Let me show you how patience works with us and our children and how everything I said will make sense to you and it will make you relate to God in a split of a second recognizing yourself in this story: We just came back from the Church on Sunday and my daughter shows me a caramel candy, you know, the brown, squishy, square one… the one that no child would be able to resist to. She got it from an old gentleman that used to bring candies for the children and used to fill them with joy. It was the tradition back in the day and he was perpetuating the Candy man legend. Our legend was Garry. And children loved him. Loved him so much that they were asking us "When do we go to Church next?". So, she put the caramel on the table and pointed to it: "Can I eat it?" At the time she was only 3 and a half. Tell me, which parent

would say "No"? And then, I had a revelation and believe it or not… I said "No". She looked at me with puppy eyes. It didn't work. She gradually changed it into the "I'm going to cry now" face… and then I told her: "If you don't eat this one, I will give you something way better. That's why I said not to eat it. But I will give it to you after we eat lunch." And you all know how children just want to skip all the meals to get to the dessert and to the candy… But she had that one right in front of her eyes, in front of her nose and her mouth. All she needed to do was to unwrap it and chew it. It was that simple… The temptation was strong. I told her: "It's your choice. You eat this one now; I don't give you what I prepared for you. You don't eat it; I will give you something way better than this one". She looked at me, put it in her palm, hold it in her fist and said: "I will wait." Do I have to remind you that these words came from a tree year old child that was told to not eat the candy she had in her hand? I was surprised to see that she's willing to do it, but I was so proud of her. What made her be patient? What made her wanting to wait even that she was having the melting candy in her fist? The fact that I told her what's happening. The fact that she knew the circumstances and the reasons why she should not do what she wanted to do so badly. The goodie that was waiting for her was the best, her favourite: the chocolate egg that comes with a toy. She loves those. By far are her favourites and I picked one up a day before in my way home from a trip. Of course I got home after they were off to bed, so I decided to give it to her the next day, after Church. And the moment came and she had another candy… So, I wanted her to not eat that candy, first of all because we needed to eat lunch, but I wanted her to be excited about what I was about to give her, not to have a little pleasure from a melting caramel candy… What did happen till the moment I told her the reason, till I made her understand what the situation was and that she will enjoy something else way better than that poor little candy that she brought from the Church? And remember: I didn't even tell her

what I would give her, but that's trust and we talked about it in another chapter. Well, you've "seen it". Her reaction was exactly how we react when we don't get things our way.

That's right. I said it. We react like babies every time when we don't get things our way and we don't think for a split of a second that maybe there is something way better in stored for us... Ok. Let me show you what I'm talking about. I am jumping from my relationship with my daughter to me... the baby and my amazing Father: God. I swear. The same situation.

Here's the story: In my line of work, which is film making and video production, I rely on computers. I bet you all know that. Especially in these days, everything has to go into and out of a computer. Well, my main computer was on the last lap, and like a good businessman, I didn't let it go until it got to the finish line. Of course I looked for something else and I found one as I wanted. What can I say? I went out of my way to get that computer: I went to another town, I got several configurations with several quotes, I paid the deposit and I was ready to go pick it up. My wife kept telling me that this is not my computer, that she has a feeling. Me? No and no and no. I ended up to be scammed of about $400 in the process and to not be able to bring the computer home... And... She was right. After several days of anger and disappointment, I learned to let it go, that I should've been patient and get one online from a reputable company and to listen to my wife's instinct. So, I looked online, I bought it online, I had it shipped to me and I didn't have to move a finger. It came in 2 days instead of one week and it came in front of the door and it came ON MY BIRTHDAY! Well, that was my chocolate egg. Do you agree?

Did you ever wonder how your behaviour would change if you'd add a little patience in the mix? How your reactions would look like, how the entire situations would change and in what

directions? I know you wished to have the understanding before anything happen, but you know: everything happens for a reason... And most of the time... we don't know the reason till later. This is how God works. And that's why we are His children... and we don't have patience. But we can learn to be patient, we can learn to understand that there is a good reason for what's happening on the moment and that we should trust that, like a good puzzle, all the pieces will come together into a beautiful image that we didn't even know it exists in the first place.

1
5

Desire

IS THAT WRONG? NO, IT'S NOT.
WHAT'S WRONG IS THE ATTITUDE WE HAVE.

Along this life we're encountered numerous moments when we desired things, when our heart was set on something and we wanted so badly that we would almost cry for it. These things are coming along and we're sucked into liking them, into desiring them and longing for them. Since we are children, and I bet you remember times when you bugged your parents in the store and even threw a temper tantrum and mopped the floors of the store with your brand new clothes hoping that they will give in and get it for you, till we are in the golden age, we keep desiring things. Is that wrong? No, it's not. What's wrong is that attitude we have towards the desire and when we realize we can't have it on the moment, right away.

Going back to that age where it was ok to throw a temper tantrum to get your way, how many times did it work? And, did you really do it? What was the reaction of your parents, of your father, when you did it? If you did throw temper tantrums when you were little, tell me: was your mom ashamed when you were doing that? Was you father annoyed or disappointed? I know you sensed their feelings and you would've stop any moment, but the desire was overwhelming and you wanted to get what you wanted. Did you get it in the end? I know there are two cases: the parents that bought your little act and as soon as you thrown yourself to the floor and start pushing yourself around with your feet, yelling, they got the thing and brought it to you and the parents that pretend they would live and ignore you or, the stronger ones, would get you up and prep you by telling you that because you did what you did you'll get it once you get home... Well, in your opinion, which set of parents you think did the right thing? Which ones do you think they were righteous? Which ones you think they mirrored God? I know you know. Exactly: the ones that would not accept the whining and would take action, that would cut the bad behaviour by showing you that it's not good what you're doing, that you're not honouring your parents by

what you're doing and that there will be consequences for your actions.

Now, if you didn't acted like that, if you didn't mop the floors screaming, but you expressed your burning desire for a thing, what did your parents do? I will say that I know already because I've been there.

Here's the story: I was in a nice country style gift shop with my daughter around Christmas. She was four at the time. We were looking around and I was letting her mainly to go around and look at things. As you know, children love to encounter new things. So, at one moment in time, she points at a Christmas Tree and shows me a beautiful red sparkly handled mirror tree decoration. I will admit it, even that I'm a grown up man, I liked it too very much. She said with a sweet begging tone: "Daddy, I would love to have this mirror in our tree, it would look so good." What can you do? Most of us would've been melted by now just by watching her doing her act. We were about a week away from decorating the tree as we planned, so I was thinking that indeed it would look nice in the tree. But, the teacher in me... said no. She looked a little bit disappointed, she put her chin down and put her lip out... she did everything she could to show me that she would've loved to have the mirror. What she did the most was that she kept calm and a respectful attitude that me and my wife nurtured into her spirit. So, she didn't throw herself down on the floor crying. That showed me that we taught her well. We left the store and got home. As soon as she got home she started to describe the decoration to my wife and make her understand that she would love to have a mirror like that for our tree. I think it was part of her strategy to win her mom on her side and then she will eventually have the mirror. What she didn't know was that when she asked me I already crafted in my mind a way to give her the mirror so her excitement would hit the highest point. And we, all parents, love when we can do that to our children, don't we?

So, I've gone back to the store, by myself, bought the mirror and kept it away from her until the day we planned to decorate the tree. And the day came, the tree was up and we filled it up with lights, candy, bulbs and decorations and when we were done, my wife went to prepare a hot chocolate just how the girls like it. Both our daughters were excited to see the tree coming together and being so bright and colourful. That was the moment when I said: "Ela, we're not done yet. You still have to add something to the tree" and I pointed to the couch where I placed the mirror for her to see. Her eyes were ecstatic, she let out a happy yell and grabbed the mirror: "This is exactly what I wished for. A mirror like this one. This is perfect! Thank you, daddy!" and she rushed to prop it on one of the branches.

Well, I could've just bought the mirror on the spot. The only thing is that by the time we would've decorate the tree she would've forget about it or become just another thing in the corner pile where all the toys and things she likes end up. But because I controlled the situation and I guided the timing and the way she would receive the thing she desired so much, now she enjoyed it for about a month every day and she will years to come because it's now in our "Christmas Tree Decoration Kit".

As I said: all our lives we desire different things. It's good to keep a humble and truthful attitude towards the situation, the desire and the one that can make it happen because if we do that, eventually we will be having in our possession all the things we desire with all our heart. You know the simple quote from the Bible that says: "ask and you shall receive". It's all in the way we ask and how we receive. It's that simple. Once we learn that, our desires will become our possessions. Not necessary on the spot, but in His timing, God's timing, remember?

Provision

Do your children ask
if you have enough money for milk?

There is a question that's lingering around for a long time and it's mostly coming from women: "What happens to men once they get married?!?" and the question is supposed to make a little fun of men because women are wondering where the studs that they met at the beginning are disappearing after marriage... what's happening to them? why are they transforming and are not the same fun guys that they were at the beginning?

The answer to that question, coming from a man, is simple: we become providers. Our entire mentality is shifting and now, that we have a marriage and soon a family, we are providers, we are the ones that want to make sure that the family has what it needs and that we, as the head of the family, are fulfilling our DUTY of providing. Because of that we're not into the fun anymore... at least not so much... we're thinking twice before going out for dinner or even when we want to go shopping. We are so into the budget and into the providing mode that we forget what attracted you, the ladies, to us in the first place: our character, our fun way to be, our spirit of adventure and so on. It is true: these things are changing us. We become stressed and we put job and work on the first place because our families are coming first all the time, but because we do that, they fall on the second place and without a reality check, we're sucked into the working whirlpool like in a black hole. We are even sacrificing family time for family's well-being. As hard as it is to understand, we do. Spending time with the family and getting called into work in the middle of a game or supper sometimes "puts the bread on the table". And this "system" is the whirlpool. The men are sinking more and more into the abyss thinking that they are doing it all and that they will bring everything to the surface once they hit the bottom.

Now, I know I advocate for the men here, but I wanted to paint you a simple picture on how men function. Do you see a little parable here? No? Ok. Here we go.

We are struggling for nothing. I know it's hard to understand. "What do you mean? All my efforts in keeping my family financially safe and everything I do is for nothing?" No. Your efforts are admirable, but, imagine having your toddlers one morning worrying and not knowing what to do, running around like a chicken with no heads, whining and starting a whole apocalyptic scene because there is no milk in the house. Right? You'd think: "Why are they worrying? I will go buy some" but they don't want to listen to you and they keep going crazy like the world will end. Well... this is our strive. We do provide and it's a noble thing to do. That's what it makes a good father, one that takes care of his family and loves them so much that he would do anything just to make sure that they are taking care of. Some classic authors treated the subject... you know them.

Exactly how we are doing our best to provide, in the same way God has everything for us. He provides everything for us as long as we know how to ask and as long as we don't worry. It's a fragile balance, but it is there and it is true. Remember: God wants us to be like the toddlers that don't have to worry if there are enough diapers or milk, or food or anything else. He wants us to enjoy life and enjoy our family exactly how you want your children to enjoy their lives and to be children, to enjoy their toys and their pets, their brothers and sisters, their room and everything you provide for them. Do they ask you if you have enough money for milk? Do they ask you if you got a raise? Do they ask you if you'll get a second job to pay for their college? No. They are enjoying life because they are being blessed with your provision... just like you are being blessed with God's provision. You just have hit the brakes and trust Him.

**1
7**

Complaining

AT THE END OF EVERY TASK THERE IS A REWARD. EVERY SINGLE TIME.

Hold on to your seats! This is one of the most common actions that we do even if we don't have reasons.

I bet we all know what it means... I don't know if we do have the right or not to complain... but we all complain. Small complains, big complains about small or big things, we do complain... It's so hard to keep it in and not do that in the duration of our lives. I have to admit it: I used to complain a lot at times... I still do it, but I can say I cut 90% of it. That's because, once I understood that God is our father, we are complaining children... And becoming a father with complaining children... I noticed the similarity and decided to change. I think that by becoming fathers we change our perspective on life and, we want it or not, we grow our relationship with God.

Here's a story:

Fall time. Our place. Backyard. Me and my three year old we're enjoying the last warmth of the sun before the winter... an Indian summer. Beautiful. The walnut trees shed their leaves and of course their nuts and it was about time to gather them. So, I decided to do it right there and then. I brought a contractor bucket and started to pick them off the grass and throw them in the bucket. Ela started to "help" me by picking one up and by the time she would get to the bucket she would drop it several times, but her intention was beautiful. That made me think of a game: "You fill up the bucket, you get candies. What do you think?" Of course, excitement, loud excitement. Done deal. I laid out the rules: "Get the nuts off the ground and when you fill up the bucket I will give you candies" Of course, when you bring candies into a discussion with children, all the other things are blacked out. I went into the house to bring the candies out and left her picking walnuts. When I came out she yelled "I'm done!" I was really surprised. I knew for sure I wasn't distracted by anything inside, I didn't stop to watch TV or anything else, so I didn't spend too much time inside... Hmmm... Ok. I went to look at the bucket: the walnuts were laying there, just two of them. I turned to her and explained to her again: "You need to fill up the bucket, which means you need to bring a lot of nuts until they reach this level and that means that the bucket is full. You have to not be able to fit another walnut in the bucket". She got it. This time she knows what she has to do. So she's going straight to a walnut she put her eyes on while I was still explaining to her what she needs to do, picks it up, finds another two right close to that one, gets them all in her hands and comes back running throwing them in the buckets while she was still running. "I'm done!" She smiles at me and expects the candy. I thought she got the idea but it looks like she didn't. I tell her "Honey, bring another walnut to see if you can fit it in the bucket. Let's see if you can" and she's just making one step, picks up a nut that she dropped earlier and throws it in the bucket with an annoyed "I'm done" that meant more "Live me alone. I am done for good. I am not doing this anymore" and she asked me like she was sent by the mob to collect the protection fee: "Where's the candy?". Inside, I was laughing with tears... but I couldn't show her that she's cute and funny because I didn't want her to get the wrong idea so I told her "Sweetie, you get the candy if you finish the job..." Well, annoyed, she turned around and starts looking for other nuts... but this time she wasn't excited any more... it was work, not fun anymore. She brought another two nuts, dropped them in the bucket like some rotten eggs and gave me the line "I'm done" crossing her arms. Angry. I will be honest... I think I even felt a tint of hate in that stance. That made me want to help her a little bit, so I went in the shed and I brought out a little bucket and made a proposal: "Ok. Take this little bucket, fill it up, dump it in the big bucket and in this way it will be a lot easier for you and you can finish faster". So she takes the little bucket, fills it up and, not even bringing it back, yells "I'm done". This time with a smile or her face because she really filled up a bucket... but it was the wrong one. "No sweetie, you take the little

bucket, fill it up, bring it to dump it in the big bucket and when you fill up the big bucket, then you get the candy." Again she starts complaining. She even thrown away the little bucket with anger... and that was the moment when I had a revelation: Wow! If we do this to God, we should consider even being lucky we're still alive...

The wrath you feel growing inside when you say "Sweetie, I'll give you candy, just do this task" and you watch the entire episode unfolding in front of you and the aggravation that comes with it, the complaining that grows every step of the task... and ending up not completing the task and you being the bad guy in their eyes, is what made me think "this is how God feels when we keep complaining even after He's giving us tools and even help?". The task wasn't hard to accomplish. As you know, I know to weight my daughter's capabilities and, even that I push her sometimes a little bit, I am not going overboard. All she had to do was to fill up a bucket with nuts. It wasn't an industrial bin, or a train wagon... just a bucket. And I even helped her "optimize her workflow" and on top of that I brought the candy outside so she can have an eye on the reward and be motivated to finish quick. In my mind I got so angry... and I was thinking "we anger God so much but He loves us so much" and yes, I was angry towards what she was doing, complaining all the time, not towards her as a person, loving her even then, I didn't stop loving her a moment. But do you know, and here I talk to the fathers, those moments when... sometimes... your children are upsetting you so much, anger you so much that you're shaking? Ok. Imagine that God feels the same way when we just keep complaining... keep complaining... at every step. Did you ever wonder why we're not getting the rewards a lot of times? It's because God is waiting for us to finish the task.... but... we keep complaining and keep procrastinating... because of the complaining.

Complain is the opposite of obedience. Obedience means "Yes Sir! I'll do whatever you ask me" no other comments or anything else... Just do it. When you finish you're like "Here I am, I'm done"... and THEN you get the reward. That's it.

The funny thing is that this is happening even in a job. A lot of people that are employees don't do anything else but complain about their job, the complaint gets to the point where they don't do the job right anymore and the products that they are making, not being up to par, can't be sold by the boss, the owner of the business, can't make the profit and because of that... doesn't have the money to pay the salary of the one that complained about the job in the first place... the vicious cycle crushes on the complainer and the bad guy is the boss with no guilt... the boss that hired the one that was looking for a job, handed the resume, got the interview and was happy to get the job. Do I have to tell you how this applies to God? I think you got it and I bet you got the idea that is good to step back and re-assess the situation, re-think who's to blame here and if we have any reasons to complain at all in some situations. I know that a lot of times we don't understand why we have to go through some stages and we need to endure some situations, but they are all a tiny part of the "big picture". From our perspective, the thing we're complaining about is the big as the world, but from God's perspective is just a little piece of the puzzle that you have to figure how it fits in the "big picture" and once you do that you'll learn to understand that it's no use to complain, but to look forward for the reward of being obedient. At the end of every task there is a reward. Every time.

Complaining, complaining, complaining...

I think we should get over this. We should grow up and get over it. I know that God wants that from us... Not necessary grow but, but get over the whining stage of our lives.

1
8

Disobedience

So, this is how we, the human beings, are wired. We, from babies to Presidents, don't like to listen to warnings or advice.

And... another question.

Tell me please: how do you feel when you tell your children to not touch something and they still do in spite of you telling them that they might be punished if they do?

Again: I am talking with the fathers but, if you're a teenage boy and you're wondering, try to relate with the story by identifying yourself as the child in the story and a future father. You'll gonna understand a lot.

Let's say you bought yourself a brand new laptop and you transferred all your data from the old one which you got rid of. You have now a powerful machine, you have all your files nice in order and everything is finally in its place after a not so peaceful process of transferring and cleaning everything, organizing and discarding what you don't need, making sure you keep the useful files and programs and everything that comes with a migration like this... not an easy process. Let's say that right now you're doing a backup to make sure you're safe. This kind of process takes a while. During this process is crucial you don't do anything else so it completes successfully.

So, you're in the kitchen, your laptop is on the table, you are going to get yourself a nice cold drink from the fridge and your children are running in... and you know how children run: with a lot of energy and enthusiasm. At that moment they don't care about your laptop or even about you... they are just running around the table, maybe playing catch, laughing and screaming. They don't bother you because you know they are children and they need to burn their energy somehow. But, to be on the safe side... you're telling them: "Careful! Do not touch the laptop." And... this is when you really stirred up their curiosity because until then... they didn't even noticed it. They look at you, they look at the

laptop and they start to get curious now... You, as a good father, are giving them the reason why they shouldn't touch it: "I don't want to lose my files". They got the idea, or at least you think they got it, and they resume their game running around and yelling with enthusiasm.

Figuring that the process will take a while, but still wanting to be around in case it finishes earlier than you expected, you go in the living room to watch some TV. Your children are running all around the house. They are having fun. It doesn't bother you... in fact you're content and pleased that they are having fun.

Suddenly, they get quiet. You don't hear them anymore. They are not running or yelling... is like they dissipated. That is weird considering the energy they were having. So, you get off the couch and look around... and what do you see? They are on the chair in front of your laptop... pushing buttons.

Tell me: how do you feel?

You know you TOLD them NOT to touch it!

Of course you dash to them and when you get to see your screen you notice that your laptop is formatting everything you have, which means you lost all your work files, your pictures and so on. Don't ask me how they did it... you know children do things. Now remember: this is just an illustration, a made up case to underline the point I want to make.

So, again: what do you feel? How do you feel in that moment? First of all you're disappointed because they didn't listen to you, they didn't respect your word and your authority, you feel angered because, at that point, you realized that there will be some changes in your life, some changes that will not be good because you lost your files and the anger doubles because they

didn't even take the blame, they just ran away and hide. Hmmm... That's a lot of anger right there. Now, tell me something: in that anger moments... what would you like to do to them? Right on the spot... you want to punish them. You are upset, angered, infuriated of the situation. You were minding your business being content that you have a new machine and that all your "ducks" are falling nice in a row and, you know... life was good. But now... the anger takes over. Well, you don't want to beat them up, but you would like to discipline them to show them that what they did was wrong and that not listening to you is wrong and these come with consequences. But by the time you get to them, you start to calm down and understand that children don't understand life as adults do, they have another set of values, so you want to "talk some sense in them", make them understand what they did wrong and why it is wrong. So, trying to restrain your anger, you sit them down and, still with an angry tone, a smoldered one, you try to explain to them the gravity of the situation. But they don't understand. What they understand is that you're angry. That's it. They don't understand that you might lose your business or your job because of that, you lose the income and because of that, you might have to scale down which means you might have to move in a smaller place, they will lose their friends, you might not have the same car and so and so. And the most important thing they don't understand is that they triggered the change. And all that... just by not listening to you.

Does that sound familiar? Maybe it happens to some of you. Not necessary just like in my example, but a similar story. Let me just give you a hint: someone, at one point in time, ate an apple. It wasn't you or Jobs, or Newton... yep, it was Eve in the garden of Eden as the Bible says. And, as you know, God told them to not touch the forbidden fruit... and they did. And what happen after that? Just like in my story, God got angry and Adam and Eve hid just like the children and when God found them, He punished

them by banishing them from the garden. And God is a good father. Could he do a lot more worse than that? Could he just evaporate them out of existence? He could've done a lot more than just tell them to go and find a way of redemption. But, because He loved them, He showed them what they did wrong and give them the free will to repent, straighten up and make things right. Imagine if God wouldn't punish them at that time. What would it happen? They would've push the boundaries by doing more and more and trying more things that they shouldn't supposed to, wrong things. And they would've become more disobedient and, in time deny God as their father, as their Creator.

So, this is how we, the human beings, are wired. We, from babies to Presidents, don't like to listen to warnings or advice and that's what creates drama which triggers wrath and anger and punishment... things that shouldn't be in this world. If the Ten Commandments would be kept sacred by all people, honouring our parents would be a priority and it would be easy and this world would live in harmony.

It all starts with obedience.

Free Will

EVERY TIME WHEN SOMEONE DOES SOMETHING WRONG.
IN THE MOMENT THEY THINK OF DOING IT.
BEFORE THEY DO IT.
THEY KNOW IS WRONG.

Everyone, as a person, has free will. We all know that. "But what is fee will?" you gonna ask.

Is just my will of doing whatever I want? Freely? Is my will of doing good or evil? Doesn't matter what... is my free will? "It's my life, I can do whatever I want with it" kind of attitude? WHAT IS the free will?

Well, let me illustrate it to you thought a little story. So, I bought my little girl a bicycle and, to enhance her experience, I got her a little horn. I didn't install it right away on the bike because I got caught up with work so the horn, in a magical way, got into her room. How did I find out? She was blowing that horn to the point of despair. It was getting so annoying... but she was loving it. She was about three year old at the time and the sound that horn made (pretty loud) and the fact that she was triggering that sound was giving her a lot of joy. It didn't matter if it was quiet time, play time or any other time, when she could get it in her hands, there was another horn session! Lots of noise and joy upstairs and frustration downstairs. So, I went upstairs and, with a good fatherly tone, I said to my little three year old: "Listen, I do understand that you like this horn, but I want you to understand that you have the free will to use it whenever you feel that is ok to use it." So, I didn't go upstairs and yank it off her hands and say "You're a bad girl! You're annoying me with this loud horn! Stop it! I think I will throw it in the garbage." and so on. Again, I just sat her down and I said: "If you want to use it, do it when you think it's right".

Remember: she was only three years old. To my surprise, since our little talk, she would come and look at me and at mommy, and just by watching us and what we do, like watching TV or being on the phone or reading a book or other quiet things, she knew not to blow the horn. Or, sometimes, she would try to play with it

upstairs and try to not be too loud. I was hearing how she would try to pump it but not go full blast.

For me, it was shocking how children can understand the free will right away. Right away! So we have the free will programed in us.

So God gave us the free will so we can understand our limits, what is good to do, to understand our own conscience and what to do with it. It is so simple. Just try that with your children. Sit them down and talk to them almost like with a grown up and explain to them that you don't forbid them to do something, you're just asking them to do it the right way. And talking about the right way, we do have in our DNA, in our consciousness, in our spirit, in our soul, we have embedded, beside the free will, the good will... and I will tell you how I know that.

Every time when you want to do something that you know is not right, every time when someone does something wrong, in the moment they think of doing it, before they do it, they know is wrong. How amazing is that? So, before you do something, leave a beat, take a step back and see if it feels right. By doing that you're exercising your free will by not jumping into wrong decisions in the wrong moments.

We are built on the most pure foundation, principles and rules, the most pure thoughts and actions and that stays with us our entire life. What we do, the path we take, is dictated by our free will.

20

Rules

THEY SET BOUNDARIES AND THEY LIMIT BEHAVIORS THAT,
UNCONTROLLED, THEY CAN BECOME A LIFE STYLE
THAT WILL LEAD THE CHILD ON THE WRONG PATH.

Like any other thing in this world, people are governed by rules. If you want to play a good game, you have to obey the rules. As soon as someone breaks the rules, it's not a fun game anymore... and ironically, even the games with no rules have one rule: "there's no rules".

So, going to the children, rules are important in their development. Rules are giving them structure and eventually are guiding them in taking the right decisions and use their free will wisely and responsibly. Rules tells them who's in charge and who they should listen to, they tell them what they are allowed and what not, they set boundaries and they limit behaviours that, uncontrolled, they can become a life style that will lead the child on the wrong path.

Remember the title of the book? Exactly. We are God's children. He is our father. Because of that, he installed a set of rules for all of us, for the mankind, to follow and obey so we can function proper and be able to reach harmony and develop to our full potential. Why did He do that? Because He loves us and He wants us to have the best in life, to have the best life. We all do. Once we become fathers, good fathers, we all want our children to have the best, even things that we never had, we all want our children to become someone and to be respected, loved and cherished, we all want only the best for them...

And to make sure they will get there, we are setting up rules so they can stay safe first of all: don't touch the stove, don't jump there, don't put your fingers in there, don't touch the knife, don't run with scissors... and so on. Do we do that because we are so mean that we want them to not be able to do anything? Nope... We just want to make sure they will be safe and they will not hurt themselves. We don't like to see our children suffer, don't we? We can't stand when a child hurts, physically or emotional. We

are nurturers by design. If you didn't notice... we even change the tone when we talk to our children.

So, you set rules to ensure that they will grow up and they will be shaped and polished by your household set of values, "by your rules".

I know you know it already... I know you know where I'm going and I will say just this:

The Ten Commandments.

1. You shall have no other gods before Me.
2. You shall not make idols.
3. You shall not take the name of the LORD your God in vain.
4. Remember the Sabbath day, to keep it holy.
5. Honor your father and your mother.
6. You shall not murder.
7. You shall not commit adultery.
8. You shall not steal.
9. You shall not bear false witness against your neighbour.
10. You shall not covet.

Have a look at them and tell me: what kind of world would this be if we'd respect all these rules? Really. Please answer yourselves and you can even voice it. No one will hear you. Now take those commandments and apply them to you. I am serious. Pretend that you are the one that wrote them and see if they apply in your household. Would that be the main rules that should govern the raising of your children? After these ones there should be the "do not touch" ones.

You see how simple it is? Do you see how you don't have to be religious or any other "type of people" to follow something that

has common sense, something that is so real and so simple that is impossible to not want to respect and follow.

To make it easier for you, here's the Ten Commandments applied to a family and their children:

1. You shall have no **other parents than us**
2. You shall not **go and listen to others over your parents.**
3. You shall not take the name of the **parents** in vain.
4. Remember the Sabbath day, to keep it holy.
5. **Honor your father and your mother.**
6. You shall not **bully, hurt, swear, murder.**
7. You shall not **cheat, double cross, be mischievous, be sneaky.**
8. You shall not **steal.**
9. You shall not **lie to hurt someone's feelings.**
10. You shall not **desire things that are not yours or are not meant for you.**

By the way: I didn't excluded God from the Ten Commandments, I just wanted to show you how, if you relate to them, they are so applicable. What do you think? Is this an eye opener? Is it simple? I know. It's so simple, it's hard to understand that it's been so many years right under our noses and we just look at them, maybe even quote them, we are letting them pass by just like words in the wind... and we don't look into the meaning of them and how, if we apply them, they make our lives, our family life, so much better.

Plans

CHILDREN. A LOT OF TIMES
TAKE THE PLACE OF YOUR
OLD PLANS AND VISIONS.

Let's talk about plans.

You know, when you are growing up, you want to become somebody. You want to become somebody socially, in your career and in your family. You have plans. Now, when you're becoming a father, you start making plans for your children... You see... in the moment when you become a father you feel like an extension of you, with everything that you are, is coming into this world and you feel to nurture it and you feel that the newborn, your extension, will carry you, your visions, your dreams forward. So you have plans for your children, you have dreams, you hope they will be able to accomplish things, became someone, carry your family line, culture, traditions, your roots, your personality, complete you and your carry existence forward.

How do you feel now, when you don't have children? You feel like you're on the top of the world, like the world is yours, like is just you and your plans and most of the times the plans are... selfish. I don't blame you. We all go through that. It's normal. We are human beings that are taught to take life and run with it and sometimes... run off it by running away from responsibility, by not taking the certain roles that we were design for: like being a father.

Once you become a father, that selfishness, gradually, because it doesn't happen in an instant, disappears. Why? It's because that's what a father does, he puts he's needs last, behind his family and children. Always. All the time he has plans for his children. A good father has the best for his children and that's why he looks for ways on how his children can become successful.

Now, for the ones that are parents: fathers, am I right? Isn't that once you became a father your world changed and even your plans changed and maybe, in some cases, it was tough to realize

that, to realize that you, as a person, are not just one anymore and that your plans, your dreams and your visions include your children and a lot of times they take the place of your old plans and visions. My point is that as soon as you become a father, a good one, you start to prioritize and to think of the well-being of your family and your children. Don't tell me that you didn't think, while holding those tiny babies in your arms, that it would be nice for them to become successful actors, doctors, athletes and mostly thoughts that relate with your dreams that you had before having a family.

Step by step, you are planning and looking more and more in the future. As they are growing up, you starting to think on how you want to send them to college, how you want them to get some specific careers and it's nothing wrong about it, it's just you wanting the best for your children, it's not that your plans will be their plans. You just dare to think and dream of their future.

As you see... you care. If in your mind, you are having plans for your children and for their future, you care! And that's what a good father does. That's what God does for each one of us. It's just that everything is happening in His timing and we don't know about each stage of his plan, exactly how our children don't know about the college we want to send them to. Try and talk to your two year old and tell them that you want to send them to college to study, let's say architecture, and to explain to them that it would be a good career considering the economic environment, the beauty and the romance of the trade, the accomplishment feeling that they will get when they see that an idea from their minds got on the drawing board and into a full size building and what you'll get back from them it will be: "Dada" and maybe a smile. That's because they don't understand. It's the same thing. We wouldn't be able to understand God's plan for us, but we can trust that He has a good plan... just like we do for our children.

2
2

Helping Help

YEP, YOUR CHILDREN TREATED YOU LIKE A SUCKER:
USED YOU AND DUMPED YOU.

I'm talking with the fathers here and of course, for you guys that are not fathers yet, this is a fun side of being a father because you'll not gonna believe what's happening sometimes. And... let me tell you how.

How do you feel when your children are asking you for your help?

Ok, ok... You might do something important at the time and suddenly they come yelling and they do whatever they can to get your attention and they are asking for your help in what they do. Of course you, as a good father, drop everything off and you go to see what's the situation, what they need help with and as soon as you get there you already know how things are, what it needs to be done because you are a grown up with experience and knowledge and you know that what it looks impossible to them it might be really simple for you. So you get there and you start helping. Let's say it was a toy that needed some parts re-assembled. You start putting the pieces together and you trying to do your best to help them and in the middle of the process you realize that... you are the only one that does the work and you throw them the "hey, you don't want to help me help you?" kind of look and they don't get it and after that you look at them again and you make them a sign to come close to you to help put everything together because they asked for your help, but they don't do anything. They get the hint and start helping you by passing you pieces and maybe tools you'd need, if they know what is needed. And you're getting again into it and more concentrated to finish it so you can get back to what you were doing if you didn't forgot by now what was you were doing in the first place. After a while, when you're getting closer to finish assembling the thing, you raise your eyes and you notice that they are not even there anymore. They found another project already or they just got distracted and they are playing somewhere in another room or even in the backyard... And you, the sucker, are caught in there, doing all the work for them, finishing their

"problem", resolving the situation, dropping everything you were doing before, something that maybe was way more important than this and you just realized that you are a sucker. He he... Yep, your children treated you like a sucker: used you and dumped you. How does that feel? So, I am talking to you, fathers: now if you're looking back at those kind of moments you are smiling. But, man, right in that moment... you just wanted to grab something and give it to them... you know... in your mind. He he he... You just wanted to call them and discipline them, call them and explain them that is not nice, that when you ask for help when you have a problem, you are the one that deals with the problem and stay there to help the one that helps you, you're not just vanishing with no trace leaving the helper do all the work while you're playing somewhere else.

Do you recognize yourself? This is what we, the grown-ups, do... a lot of times. We ask God to help us with something and we expect Him to do all the work. A lot of times we just pray and forget about it, stop doing anything about the situation anymore, because God will take care of it. But God wants us there, wants us to be part of the healing, of the remedy, of the solution, not for us to move on and move out. How do you think God feels when we do that, when we leave him alone with our problems instead of being there with him, listening to His guidance and accepting His help in an active way? Now you know how... is that simple.

For you, my dear future fathers, it's good that you're reading this book because it will help you become good fathers and you'll learn that patience and guidance are the main qualities when dealing with children. It's good to know that your children are children and you love them unconditionally, just like God loves us...

Scraping By

A LOT OF THE GOOD OPPORTUNITIES
THAT WE SHOULD TAKE
ARE RIGHT UNDER OUR NOSES

We are guilty of it. We are.

So many times in our lives we felt like we're just scraping by and that we don't have any chance in anything, that we are bound to do that all our lives and to be locked into a vicious cycle that swallows our lives slowly. I admit it. I was there... until I let go, until I put my head up and I said to myself that there has to be a better way, that this is not meant for me. We are so blessed to have such a good father, we don't even know it. And the funny thing is that a lot of the good opportunities that we should take are right under our noses but we don't act on them. It might be because we're too busy scraping or too afraid that we'll lose even the scraping.

Here's a simple example that made me think of this:

I love stir fry! I do! Is one of my favourite food: great variety of flavour and easy to make and if it has shrimp in it, I am just loving it! Ok. Why I say that? We were having lunch and we were enjoying some shrimp stir fry in the family. Around the table. All four of us. Everyone quiet because you couldn't sneak a word in there... this is how good it was. So, we are getting close to finish and Ela, three at the time started to suck on the shrimp tales. She loves shrimp stir fry too... Can you tell? Ok. So, she was doing that and until I realized what she was doing she went through most of them. I asked her "why do you do that?" She said that she doesn't have shrimp any more so she's trying to get the most of it... Remember: three years old. I smiled and I got one of my jumbo shrimps off my plate into my fork and I placed it in front of her. To my surprise, she didn't see it. I was shocked... and amused. The big shrimp was hanging about ten inches in front of her face but she was way too busy on sucking on those tales that she didn't want to raise her eyes to have a look at that juicy shrimp that was waiting for her to sink her teeth into. I was sitting there, holding

the fork and eventually I lowered it and she saw it, made some big eyes dropped the tale and jumped on fresh new "catch". And guess what? Once she was done with that one, I gave her another one. I nudged my wife to look at the situation. She smiled and that made her realized that I am right when I say that we, the humans, do the same thing: we scrape by not looking for the opportunity and the open doors that God has for us.

Yes, God has opportunities laid in front of us every single day. It's up to us to want to see them and act upon them, and, be grateful for them. All we need to do, is to take a break from scraping and look around with eyes wide open.

2
4

Praise

IS ONE OF THE MOST OVERWHELMING FEELINGS
YOU'LL HAVE IN YOUR LIFE

Tell me something: if you're a parent or not, but if you're a parent, tell me if you're relating to this.

How do you feel when, out of the blue, your children come to you and say: "Daddy, I love you"? It doesn't matter the age. They can be just learning to talk or it can be beside your bed on your last breath. How does it feel? You didn't ask them to say it, you didn't do anything special to get them so excited that they had to say it, you didn't expect it, you didn't give them any signs that you wanted them to say that, you were just there and they just came to you and said "I love you" and gave you a hug. How do you feel in that moment?

I think you're falling in love again, you're feeling praised, you're feeling loved, you're feeling like you did a good job, like you are a good father, like you are worthy of your children, you're melting, especially if they their age is one digit because you didn't expect at all for them to do something like this. You're feeling overwhelmed sometimes... and depending on your age and their age, you might even share a tear that you might hide it or show it with pride. Why? It's because you're being praised out of the blue, with no command, no desire, no other triggers, nothing but pure love. Just because they feel so much love for you they just wanted to come and tell you and show you what they feel for you. How beautiful it is to be praised by your own children! How beautiful is that! Now that's something that makes you feel like a good father and that you did something good by putting all the hard work, the time, the dedication, the love and passion in raising your children and teach them to mirror you.

I know you know where I'm going with this. This is how you make God feel when you praise Him, when you love him, when you really pray to him, and that prayer is not in that "God give me" line, but is a genuine prayer, you know, the one when you are

grateful for His love and thankful for everything He's doing for you. Through prayer you acknowledge that you have His favour, that you love him and a true prayer come from your heart, comes from your desire to be grateful, to seize the moment and let Him know you love Him. How do you think He feels when, out of the blue, you just whisper "Thank you, God!" or "I love you, God" or "God, I praise you and give you all the Glory".

I do hope you relate to this and that you feel how God feels. Having your children coming to you from nowhere with no warnings and hug you and say "I love you, daddy" is praise and is one of the most overwhelming feelings you'll have in your life.

**2
5**

Separation

PARENTS TREAT THE TEENS LIKE CHILDREN.
TEENS WANTING TO BE TREATED LIKE ADULTS.
THERE'S THE CONFLICT AND THE SEPARATION.

This is for students and not just for them but for the fathers and grandfathers because I know all of you, at one point, you'll agree with me. Why I am saying that you will agree with me is because everyone, including me, we reach one point in our life when we... grow up. We are not the babies, the toddlers and the children we used to be. We are changing in the thinking, in behaviour, physically, we are becoming another person all together. Only our strong foundation that our parents lay for us remains intact in our being, but in rest... we are almost another person. We are maturing. Yes, it's true, some of us a little bit earlier, some of us later, but we are all reaching that point when we think we are there, we are mature, even that we didn't reach the age of maturity. We think that our mind, our thinking reached the maturity stage. From that moment on, we think that we can do all things all by ourselves, that we don't need our parents any more, we even start to ridicule our parents and sometimes we even get to the point where we are ashamed to be seen with them around or with them even hugging us and loving us how they did from our first moment in this world. And that, step by step, in some cases, goes even farther into not honouring them any more by not being obedient, by talking back, by doing little stupid things that we shouldn't do. I am not pointing fingers... we all gone through it, so you're ok.

How do you think your parents feel when you reach that moments?
I bet they are happy to see you growing and coming up with your own ideas and concepts, seeing that you start to become independent and responsible, that you're starting to act like an adult, even that you're not one yet. They are proud of you and they love you even more! The only thing is that they start to get annoyed by your behaviour because you think they are against you because they still treat you with the same tenderness and

love that you usually give to a child... while you want to be treated like an adult.

Parents and grandparents: you know you've been there too... I am talking about the little rebellion when your parents were trying to show you love when you were a teenager. The only thing is that growing up, becoming a parent and growing old, you start to understand your parents more and more and you become your parents... How many times did you find yourselves in a place where, after you said something to your teens, you realized that you sound just like your parents? So, starting to understand your parents, you see that them showing you love while you were a teen... wasn't a bad thing and they weren't trying to embarrass you, but just treat you as they always did: with love.

So, the children grow up and now, being teens, they are not kids anymore, but not adults yet. If you're a teen, you know the feeling... and, once again: we all been there. So, parents treat the teens like children, teen wanting to be treated like adults. There's the conflict and there's the separation. This conflict pushes the teens to go from the family set to the entourage one and starting to feel more comfortable with the peers because "they understand". Some of the teens end up in a bad entourage like gangs that are up to no go that don't want the betterment of the new teen, but the embarrassment through the initiation and the guilt by being pushed to do things against the principals and values learned at home. As a parent, you are disappointed because you don't want your child to end up like that... so, let's not go so extreme. Let's say your son or daughter have a nice circle of friends and they spend more time with them than with you, and when you come around, even that you try to be the cool parent, they are still embarrassed with you.

You, the teens: am I right with what I'm saying here? Do you identify yourself with at least a little bit of this? Do you see how

you push away from the parents trying to become an adult even that you're not yet one, trying to limit your parent's role in your life? How many of you that you read or hear this message went back to their parents? Did you go back because you wanted or because you were forced to go back because you didn't make it by yourself, because you hit a wall, you were betrayed, because you've been hurt, because you got in trouble, because the world disappointed you? How many of you? If you admit you're one, that's good. You are becoming an adult. Admitting your mistakes is part of being an adult.

To those who went away from the parents for a period of time: how did your parents reacted when they saw you coming back? Did they look at you with love? Did they open their arms? Did they open their door? Were they happy to see you healthy, to see you're ok? Were they happy to see you? I think they were. Why? Because they are parents and parents, especially good parents, love their children no matter what for the rest of their lives. Did you know that a lot of times parents have the urge to run after you and bring you home, that they have the urge to follow you step by step to make sure you're ok? But they don't do it because they know you are going through the teen stage which is a confusing one and you need to find the way and you need your space. Parents understand that. You will too, once you become one.

Just picture how you are being waited for by God. We all know that life is pretty confusing sometimes and we think we can do it all by ourselves and that we don't need our father's help, that we figured everything out and we're invincible... and still... God is waiting... patiently because He knows that eventually, even on your last breath, you'll go back to Him because He's a good father... so treat Him like one.

Deserted

HE WILL LET YOU SEE HOW IT FEELS TO BE DESERTED
AND TO UNDERSTAND THAT IT IS GOOD TO KEEP CLOSE
AND IN CONTACT AT ALL TIMES

At times we tend to run and to run fast in our lives. We forget that live should be a beautiful stroll in the park with sunshine, butterflies and all the beautiful things that surrender us. I know you'll say that I am way to out of it now just because I mention simple things that we're not paying attention to anymore. But think of the times when you had the chance to go for a walk with your father, and if you didn't, let me share with you the feeling.

This time the story goes both ways: me and my dad and me and my girls. Going for walks in the park was always fun because I knew we'll always end up in the playground and I would play around with the other children while my father would talk to the other parents. It was good times and it was good times because he would carve time from his sleeping time, because he was working shift work, and instead of getting his rest, he would go walking with me. It's amazing how, us as children, never understand at the time the sacrifices our parents make for us to make sure we're having a good childhood. So, where am I going with this? Well, sometimes, and mostly when we would go to a shop to get something, maybe in a grocery store, I tended to go around and lose focus on the fact that I was with my father, but start the adventure of finding sweets. You know... like any other child. Now... how many times did that happen to you? You know, to wander around and lose sight of your parents and thinking that you're deserted, that you'll not going to see them again and that from that moment on... you're alone? Several, I know. It happens to all of us. The thing is that you weren't deserted, and we'll talk about that a little bit later, but you just wandered away from your parent and you got lost... at a certain level, because being lost for good means you wouldn't be found anymore. But this is what you think at that moment the level of the situation is at: you're lost for good. And what did you do in those desperate moments? You started to panic and cry so hard that you wouldn't be able to see clear anymore because the tears would blur your vision.

In those moments, and here we'll talk about being deserted, a good father would let you cry for a while so you understand the gravity of the situation when you wander like that and you just lose contact. He will let you see how it feels to be deserted and to understand that it is good to keep close and in contact at all times. I will not say that a mom would do that because we all know a mom wouldn't have the heart for that. But a good father will have the strength to do it. Now, that's ok to test your children a little bit, "freak them out" so they know to not do it next time, but we know there are parents that did the "Mall Move" where they took their child and telling them to wait in a spot invoking a reason, they just left not looking back ditching and scarring the child for life. I am sorry if that happen to you. If you're reading this book, you're strong and you grew up just the way you wanted and you've done the right choices. I am proud of you and we all are proud of you, all of us that know your story.

So, as I was saying, a good father would test the child. Mine did... and, oh boy, did I cry like a little girl or what? I remember the panic and the disorientation, I remember not being able to see in front of my eye, like an instant cataract conquered my sight, I remember how my body temperature raised abruptly and how I was sweating... all those were the signs of feeling deserted. At the moment I didn't know what was happening to me, I didn't know it was my fault, I didn't know what will it happen next and the most important: where did my dad vanished? He was at the end of the isle, watching me with his arms crossed... and he even told me that I was looking his direction, but I couldn't see him. Of course he came to me and got me in his arms and assured me that he's there and that I am ok, but in the same time he let me know that this is happening because of me and that he wanted to show me how it is to not listen and to not wanting to stick with him when we go together somewhere...

Years went by... a couple of decades... and I became a father and... my turn came to teach the same lesson. I will tell you something: it is hard. In those moments when you hear your own child crying with despair feeling deserted, our hearts are pierced with a thousand spears over and over again, but we need to be strong and let some moments go by to be able to get our children to understand that it's good for them to stay close if they want to feel secure and loved in our presence. So, the episode was for me a deja-vu, but from my father's perspective. Now I was understanding what was going on and now I was having all my questions answered in one crushing wave of feelings.

We do that as adults too... it's like we never learn. We are wandering away from God, just like we're wandering away from our parents. We are going our way in search for our "candies" and we end up in the wrong life isle, we turn around and we're blaming God that He forsaken us, that he deserted us when in fact we were just carried away by the temptations and we didn't notice that God is there all the way watching us and making sure we're safe, like a good father that He is.

2
7

Forsaken

THE GOOD PARENTS AND THE GOOD FATHERS
WILL NEVER LET THEIR CHILDREN KNOW THAT FEELING.

I'll start this one by telling you: A good father will NEVER EVER forsake his children. A good father is always there for his children, no matter in what situation they got, no matter what they did, he is there for them.

A good example... the most common one is when a teenage girl becomes pregnant. As soon as the parents find out, most of them, push her away, banish her, deny her and don't want to have anything to do with her anymore because the most important thing for them is their reputation. It's all about them, not about her. It's about how they feel: dishonoured, betrayed, embarrassed, angry and disappointed.

Now, a good parent, a good father, sees the situation, understand the mistakes, makes the child understand the mistakes and leads the child to repenting and redemption and after that, supports the child all the way. Did you noticed I said "the child"? Yes, that pregnant teen is still his child that he loves and cares about.

Another example... the son ends up in jail. Even that he was innocent... or not... he's in prison. For most of the parents it's a shame to have your son in prison. You feel the shame and judgement everywhere they go, in church, in the neighbourhood, everywhere people know your son is locked up. You look like a con family... and you never know, maybe your son was innocent or he was framed. You, as the parent, you weren't there, but as a good father you can be there for him by visiting him, by listening, by understanding what happen from his side, and again, by leading him towards redemption and by forgiving him which is a crucial component in being a good parent.

In both cases, of the girl and the boy, if the parents decided to abandon them because "they got that they deserved" they make them feel forsaken physically, mentally, emotionally and socially.

The good parents and the good fathers will never let their children know that feeling.

A lot of times parents, that don't deserve the title and the privilege of being parents, forsake their children emotionally, by fading away the compassion and the love, which makes the little ones feel lost in their loneliness. You don't know what I'm talking about? I am talking about the parents that for every little mistake they beat up that child with no mercy or forgiveness, and talking about forgiveness they keep beating them up because they don't let go. Maybe some of you've seen some cases of abuse like that on the internet and you cringed and shared some tears for that pour child abused in those videos or pictures.

Let me tell you this: a good father is there all the time for his children no matter the situation, the case, the circumstances and, of course, no matter where they end up. That is because a good father is a speckles mirror of God, whom never forsakes His children.

Sickness

WHEN WE GET SICK IT FEELS LIKE
WE'VE GROWN OLD ANOTHER FIFTY YEARS
IN TEN MINUTES

I know I am touching a subject that nobody likes, but, hey! we all going to be sick at a point in our lives. If we're sick just a little while or if we get really sick, what can we do?

How do you feel in the moment when flu hits you?... Exactly! You're feeling like you've grown old another fifty years in ten minutes. You have fever, you're tender, your muscles hurt, you move slow, you don't want to do anything, you complain, you are grumpy... all that. Those are the moments when you want to be serve by the ones around you and have a lot of compassion from everyone. Does it sound familiar? Yep...

That was for all of us, but let me tell you a little story and you'll see where I'm going. My little hyper bee... my three year old one.. reached the stage that everyone's afraid of... the terrible twos. You know babies... At the beginning you try to teach them to talk "say ma-ma, come on, you can do it... say maaa-ma" and get them to stand and walk... and you are so excited when they succeed. But, shortly after that, when they are about two-three years old, they get to their maximum annoying level when all you say is "shhhhh" and "sit". Isn't that ironic?

After being so hyper for a good period of time... she got fever... she got the flu. She didn't know what's happening with her at the moment. She didn't freak out, she understood that she was sick and the most surprising fact was that, as soon as she got the fever she started to act so normal, so adult like: she changed her behaviour, she was calm, articulating all the words, talking slow, moving soft and careful to not stumble on anything that might be in her way. In another words she grew up in a day.

The most shocking thing was that she came out of the blue to cuddle with me, she needed to feel nurtured and safe, to feel she's being taking care of. She climbed on the couch and snuggled in my chest and in that moment she went straight into my heart...

again. Then, I felt like God. Remember that at the beginning I told you that I told a group of people that I can't wait to become a father to understand God? That was the moment I almost understood Him because she came to me and at her will she wanted my presence, my safety, my love, me. That made her feel better. Yes, the medicine made her feel good physically, but emotional, the closeness was healing her.

When I had those feelings, I felt so much for God. I felt for Him because He longs for us to do that, to go to Him and be with Him, feel His presence and love, but most of the time, when we end up going to Him and looking for the comfort of His presence is when we are sick, physically and psychically. It looks like our best moments to get closer to God is when we do get sick, but what about the moments when we're healthy?

Sometimes I think that God allowed sickness in this world so we can feel to get close to Him and to learn to look for the comfort of His presence when we're healthy too, and to be grateful for our beautiful days when we don't know sickness. And what do you think God is doing then? He's just there waiting for you to want to go to Him, sick or not, to connect with Him and be close to Him, like a good father.

Journey Of Life

The most precious gift God gave us is life and today we're just zooming by it running after money and titles.

I know a lot of people are curious about the future, about what their life will be and even how it will end. Let's admit it that we all had a thought like that, but there are some people that are becoming obsessed about it and that's damaging.

Let's say you are embarking with your family for a journey to one of the most amazing places on Earth, a place where you all wanted to go. So, you're all packed and ready to go, the enthusiasm is through the roof and the excitement is loud... And here you go! On the road! Fun family! Ready to enjoy the destination... but, after a while, your children get anxious, tired of the trip, inpatient... and they start to get on your nerves with "are we there yet" when you're not even half way there. The sad part of the situation is that instead of making the best of their time by looking for landmarks, playing a game, drawing, ask questions about what they see out the window, they just complain. It is true that the goal is to get at the destination, but they don't understand that the journey to the destination is part of the adventure, is part of the vacation.

Yes, you try to distract them, so they don't bug you, with video games, movies on DVDs and other stuff, but you'd like them to enjoy the beauty you're encountering on the trip there. A lot of times when you show them a landmark and you talk about it, they are just bored and they would rather look into their little screens these days... But they should be so excited to be part of the trip, to be there with their family, exploring together, enjoying every single moment and mile of it.

And, by now, I think you got my point... We tend to overlook life trying to search for the destination. We overlook details because we just want to get there and the irony is that we don't even know where we want to get to. Do you want to know if you're in this situation? When is the last time you stopped to look at a

butterfly? I mean really stop and enjoy it's wing flapping the air in a totally out of pattern flight? When is the last time you stopped to feel the sun on your face? Really stop everything you're doing and let the light and warm nurture your being? When is the last time you stopped to listen to a bird? Not just going by, but stop and give it some time and a good listen like everything else in this world vanished? You might look at the seasons zooming by and wondering where the time flies... but the time is the same everywhere and treats everyone the same. So it's not about you not having time, it's you deciding to not have time for such small things that have no importance... at least at the moment. I've been there: I was working so much that I was seeing the seasons in time-lapse... just like in movies.

The most precious gift God gave us is life and today we're just zooming by it running after money and titles, burring ourselves in work and everything else just to wake up too late and realized that we just missed the entire journey... and we are at the destination which is just a sign in the middle of the desert saying "Exit Here".

God wants us to enjoy this gift and that's why He gives us children... to slow us down, to shift priorities and to get back at what we supposed to do from the beginning to the end: enjoy life. the moment of birth, the expectation of birth, the moment when you hold for the first time your first child, the moment when they smile to you, the moment when they first notice they pass gas, the moment when they poop and you laugh at their funny faces, the moment when they first try to say something, the moment when they cry and you don't know why, the moment when they fall asleep on you for the first time, the first word they put out... even if it wasn't a word, the first time they called you "dada", the first time when they turn, they sat, they got up on their own, the first step, the first time you caught them when they walked towards you, the moments when you teach them to do

different things like skating or biking, their first school day, the first time they leave the house because they are going on their way and the first time you became a grandparent. So never ever lose a moment because these moments are the ones that make up the journey of your life.

3
0

Death

WE ALL WANT TO KEEP LIVING.
EVEN IF IT IS ANOTHER KIND OF LIFE FORM.

Yet another subject that might get you uncomfortable... It's a subject that I'm scared of sometimes and I think it's normal to feel like that because we are living in a material world. We are trying to grow spiritual but we are embedded in matter. When we are surrounded by death, from distant places in the news, to close family, we get a little bit scared, but I will give you a little bit of hope when it comes to death.

A lot of people think that when you close your eyes for the last time in your earthy life you are gone for good, that there's nothing left anymore, that you do not exist anymore, you are gone for good and that's what scares a lot of people, including me, because we all would love our consciousness to forever perpetuate. We all want to keep living, even if it is another kind of life form, we want to go on. I wonder why we have this desire... Why we feel so strong about it? It's in us, it's a universal thought. I know you've heard about cryogenic conservation where the humans went so far that they decided to freeze their bodies or at least their heads so they can be revived in the future and continue living IF the technology evolves that much that it will allow them to do that. Another way the human race is thinking of immortality is to upload the consciousness on to a server, a cloud, and just live there because scientists today think that we are just electric pulse, just our thoughts and because of that we can just be stored somewhere in a memory block.

Back to the stage where we think that we are just these bodies and these minds and that when we get to our last breath that is the end. You see how we think? This is how a toddler thinks. Go ask a two, tree year old toddler if they know that they will grow up and if they know what they will be when they are adults, if they know if they will have families, if they know if they will go to school, if they will become parents and grandparents... well, they don't. That's because they think that the stage they are in is the life, that this is it. Their consciousness

develops in time and they become more aware of their path and life while they are growing up, more aware that they will not be toddlers all their lives. Maybe you noticed that in your life you couldn't wait to grow up. You girls, trying your mom's shoes, you guys trying to hammer a nail. You grew out of that stage, of that stage where you thought that life is just that, being a toddler. Is the same thing with death... you grow out of it, out of this material life, which is just a stage of our existence.

A little analogy: when you drive a car and you have an accident or it just gives up, you get out of the car and go get another one and move on. Did you ever think of that? That should give you some hope. Now, about the Eternal Life: Somebody promised eternal life and that someone was the most documented person in the world, with a lot of wisdom and a lot of truth and a person that did EVERYTHING he said he will do. You got it: that's Jesus. And if you remember, Jesus IS God. By God producing a son and send him in this world was the way of Him to enter the material earthy world, and He did it to show us, the people, that death is not just death, but death is just a transition and He told us exactly what is happening once we close our eyes and move on. You see how simple it is? Just look in the Bible and you'll be impressed.

3
1

Conclusion

HARMONY IN FAMILY IS WHAT GOD LIKES TO SEE
AND WHAT HE WANTS US TO BRING TO OUR FAMILIES

It's been quite a journey for me to write this book. I'll admit it that this is my first time when I author a book and let my message go on paper or displays and arrive to people around the world. As I said, I specially opted out from being edited because I wanted you to meet and get to know me through my writing. I hope you had fun reading it and that, in some instances, it open your eyes on how simple our relationship with God, our father, is and how us, the guys, are so like Him... but there is something or someone that wants to put us down and make us feel unworthy, to feel like we're not good enough so we don't even dare to think like this, like in this book.

I hope you agreed with some of my points. Again: all this came upon me in a split second and even I didn't know at that time where all that info will end up and look, it's here.

To girls, girlfriends, fiancees, wifes, mothers and even gr andmas:

If you read this book and you feel that it makes sense, now is your opportunity to help the teenage boys in your life. They are the front line in the battle for the healthy survival of your family. Share the information, the stories, support them, encourage them, let them take their father role to the full potential; get them to become good fathers and leaders. And don't stop just at them: any man that crosses your path can benefit from you reading this book.

To families with teen boys:

I hope that it inspired some of you to share it with someone that you feel needs it, that it inspired you to want to talk with your boys and share some of the ideas, that it motivated you to like and share the Facebook page [http://www.facebook.com/ourfatherbookcom] with your friends and tell them what they can discover here.

To teen boys:

If someone passed this book to you and you're reading this: CONGRATULATIONS! I don't think I would've been able to do that when I was a teen.

If you went to our website [http://www.ourfatherbook.com] or any book store, online or not, and bought the book at your free will, I ADMIRE YOU! Not too many teens these days search on how they can fulfill their main purpose in life: to become a good father.

If you're a teen dad and you are taking care of your children: YOU ARE AN INSPIRATION! Why? Not because you're a teen, because we know it wasn't quite the age to have babies, but because you ARE MAN ENOUGH to stick around, to nurture, to care and make those children feel special, to be a father figure and to be a good one.

To fathers:

If you're about to become a father for the first time in your life: brace yourself! It's a life changing experience and it will really change you for good. If you're willing to accept the change, you're one step closer to your destiny. There is a saying that once a baby comes in the family, the Heaven is opening upon your home. I know it did in mine... And I was the guy that wanted to have all his ducks in a row before children came along. It doesn't work that way. It doesn't. If your wife has the maternal instinct that it's time to have a baby, it's your duty and your destiny to let go and embrace your future. I know sometimes you're thinking that it's hard to let go to what you are and to your habits, but, once those little ones come around, I am telling you, you will be glad to drop everything for them. You can have the worst day of your life with problems at work and so on, but once you got home and those little ones did something or said something that inevitable will bring a smile on your face... you instantly forget about everything and remember that they are a huge reason to live and be victorious.

If you have teenage boys: see how you can lead by example. Remember: God leads by example and we do mirror Him... and we know by now that our children mirror us. It's installed in us. So, by being a good father, just like God, you'll be able at one point to hand them this book and let them discover how simple life is and how they can be good fathers when their turn comes.

If you ever felt like you're not a good father:

first of all... **IT'S NEVER TOO LATE!**

You can make things right and you can become the father your family wanted all along. By relating to some of the stories and understanding that we are so much like our father, God, you'll be able to be back on track in no time and even more, you will bless your family.

If you are at the stage when you start to understand your father and notice that you start to be just like him, it's time to humble yourself and go in for a big hug. If you had fights, if he ever upset you, it's time for you to really forget and make peace. As we grow older and older we realize that harmony is one of the most precious things in this world and that the harmony in family is what God likes to see and what wants us to bring to our families.

3
2

Epilogue?

I AM ABOUT TO GO ON A CRUSADE OF
INSPIRING AND MOTIVATING YOUTH
TO BECOME GOOD FATHERS

So, all this being said, I will stop here and hope that my mission is done... at least partially.

Why do I say partially? Is because I am about to go on a crusade of inspiring and motivating youth to become good fathers, to learn not to be just dads but to be fathers, to be father figures for their future children and for all the children they encounter in their lives until their last breath, to become superheroes for those little souls. I know I have it in me and I know my message will "infest" the world. I know I will be a lot on the road caring the message through my book and speeches and I am hoping that my family will understand my call and my absence.

If you think that the content of this book is worth to reach groups, anyone can book me for a motivational speaking session in school assemblies and any event. This is the direct link that you can share with event organizers:

http://bit.ly/bookflorin

or scan the QR Code

PASSING
THE
MESSAGE

INSPIRING MESSAGES AND STORIES FROM FATHERS
FROM AROUND THE WORLD
COLLECTED SPECIALLY TO MOTIVATE YOU
AND GIVE YOU HOPE.

This section came to my mind because I wished someone would've told me when I was a teen how good it is when you become a father and how wonderful it is if you're a good father for your children and a great husband to your wife. Well, in my case, I never had "all my ducks in a row" and because of that I was postponing a lot to have children. I was used to take care of myself, for myself, to build a career, to get myself some nice things, to treat myself... to be selfish. It's true that dimmed down a little bit when I met my wife, but I was going the same way. She loves to tell me that I am a workaholic... I keep telling her I need nine lives or ten clones. Anyway... when it sink to me that I am a father, that the baby I am holing is not my sister's or my cousin's I was filled of excitement! The first birth that Nadine had was a 24 hour labour, but, we didn't sleep 3 days in advance... this is how excited we were. And it comes all natural... no rehearsals, no manuals. It just overwhelms you. When they put Ela on Nadine's chest, I didn't know what to think: a little ball of purple flesh that from that moment was my daughter and I was her dad. Yes... from that moment I have someone to call me "daddy" all my life... and that makes me tear up. And... the change? I became more aggressive with what I was doing. You would think that I would just drop everything and take it easy... but no! I decided that I will work hard and play hard. Yes, the big difference is that I learned to carve time to be with my kids. I mean there are moments when I am cutting everything, shut down everything and just go and play with them for the day. And I love that! Yes, I am more responsible... I used to get in road rage from time to time and when Nadine told me "I need you to come home safe for me and for the girls" I cooled it down for good. I changed a lot and I see more and more that is because of my girls and is in better. I think God gives us kids so we can understand Him. And... I did.

Here's what fathers from around the world have to say about their experience. Enjoy and remember to pay it forward. Boys today need this a lot. Don't let them wonder blindly. Show them the light.

"Before becoming a father I was reckless, defiant, and living a very unhealthy lifestyle. I didn't realize how much my world would change until I watched my daughter enter this world and held her for the first time. All of a sudden my meaningless existence had purpose. She was so tiny, so vulnerable, so fragile, so perfect. I felt a love like I had never felt before. I realized, for her I needed to change. If I was going to be the dad I dreamed of I had to make it happen. And that meant a lot of work. It hasn't been easy and I've slipped back but for every slip back there has been more moves forward. My daughter deserves the best I can be and that is my goal."

- Morgan Schaffer, Canada - Teenage Father

"As a younger man I was crass, bold, and had a less then clean image of myself. I watched the pregnancy of my wife like a man in deep hole trying to see a beautiful sun rise. Obsessed with all that I thought I was, and all that I thought others might think of me. I was self-absorbed and a man child in many ways. The birth of my son William was an absolute truth. A beautiful truth that told me in no uncertain terms that I was more than worthy. I was his protector his provider and his stone foundation. I would never hold him or kiss him unless my hands and face were washed clean of the days filth. He was (and still is to me) a gift from God. A humbling reminder that this rare flower will someday echo my finest qualities and my faults with the same reverberation. I am a saved man and as much as I believe I'm not worthy to be saved the mere fact that I have been blessed with this task proves that I am worthy! Amen."

- Jeff Mohr, USA

"Becoming a Father when I was young, very young was scary. Looking through my teenage eyes I really feared I would ruin both of our lives, and in fear I ran from my responsibilities. I still have a lot of feeling about this   decision. I do believe all things can understood in time. However 20 years later I had another chance to be a Father, and with the confidence that I would not make the same mistakes as my past. I had much more to offer as a father as a man and would make this the very reason I live. I poured my love into my sons soul teaching him the things I've discovered along my journey and observations of life. While I continue to learn from my greatest love truest bond and the pulse of my heart, my son."

- Cary Templeman, Canada

"It happened on April 11th 2006, after a long Journey full of travel from Saudi Arabia to Lebanon passing by Bahrain full of anxiety to meet my pregnant wife Hana who was about to deliver. And here I was waiting for that moment to hold my first child, Mounya my eldest daughter. I was not sure about the feeling of being a father would be, but I was anxious to meet her.

It happened suddenly, once you hold your child in your hands, you realize that the perception about the world had changed, you feel the unconditional love and the duty to care, to love and that your role in this world has changed forever. And you start dreaming what this child would be and what would be your role accomplishing that child needs to become a great person. I feel that every day, I wake up in the morning and can't wait to check on my beautiful daughters, the four of them, that has brought so much blessing to my Wife and I, loving them and caring for them is the most important role I play in this life, and I pray God every day, to help me keep them safe, healthy and be good people."

- Ramy Boujawdeh, Lebanon

"Fatherhood graced me with the opportunity to love, hold and embrace, humanity at its best. My daughters represented hope and the spirit of new beginnings, potential and possibilities. the mystery of Christ The Vine and His branch was solved for me for Tara became the physical outcome of the spiritual fruit that God expects me to bring forth. As a father i am able to live in the hope, peace, joy and love, in a tangible way with God, myself and others; my baby child teaches me this."

- Alan McIntyre, Canada

"On becoming a Dad I never thought could Love like that before, I always felt lonely unloved. I've always been really shy & I met Erica my wife in middle school but never dated until after we graduated. After were married after a year we had our Daughter & wow it was like I captured the sun & had for my own. When you look into your Babies eyes & see her smile for the first time it washes all the hurts, disappointments away. Then when she learned to talk & calls you Daddy for the first time it's all over with you just melt & changes you again. Love is not enough a word I can say to explain how I feel for my three kids. I would gladly lay down my life for them. If you ask why I hope I do good as an ETA is to pay for my Daughter's wedding soon & help my Family finally they are my world. When you grow up poor, feeling alone & picked on all your life when you have kids that give you all their Love you want to give them all that you never had. They are my heart. That's how I was changed."

- Travis Albertson, USA

"I have never seen his eyes greener and warmer until he held our newborn daughter and later on, our son. He looked stunned, mesmerized and ready to melt away from so much happiness.

He became transparent for the first time, for it was unexpectedly easy to read his emotions...

It was then when I witnessed a turning point in his life: from the man I knew, my husband became not only our kids' protector, but mine also. He was their playmate, a mentor, a friend. He learned to respect and value a child's opinion as well as admitting that an adult (parent) can make mistakes or be wrong sometimes. That the error is human. Or that a child can actually teach you a lesson that will be hard to forget. And, what was difficult at first, he learned how to apologize to them if it happened to misjudged them. Then, how easy it is to gain their trust when they feel that they have been treated as his equals. This beautiful, complex journey made him realize that there is no greater gift than being blessed to become a father!"

- Olimpia Branzan, Canada

"Before I met my wife I used to go out and party with the guys, chase the girls, spend lots of money and "live life"... but that was just a fad... and in fact it wasn't at all living life because we were just fooling around with no purpose. Once I met my wife I started to be a little more tamed down and begun to understand that I need to grow up and be responsible, but once I became a father I became another person. Now I laugh when I look back of what I used to think life is... When I first seen my son I understood that becoming a father was in fact my destiny and that life just started for me. Until that point I was just a kid fooling around."

- Lica Ciurea, Romania

"Becoming a father has changed many things in my life I'm not just responsible for my wife and I any more, I have a family! Most important I'm always looking for opportunities to give him the best childhood he could ever ask for."

- Reno Lachapelle, Canada

"Becoming a father or Dad, was not a surprise or a difficult thing for me. Since I was a young boy, I always wanted to be married and to have a family I used to dream of having 6 children. I did not quite make it, but I now have 3. Becoming a father does require hard work and commitment.

We are fully responsible for the care and safety for our families and to do everything within our power and abilities to ensure their well-being. The commitment to love and cherish them to protect and care for them becomes your primary focus in life. Just as Jesus loved us to give his life for us. Likewise we are to give ourselves to our children."

- Stephen Graham, Canada

"When I became a father, my entire outlook on life changed. My priorities and way of life shifted. The word "love" became a whole new meaning and my reason for living never felt more real. Being a father has taught me more about life and faith than ever before."

- Stephen Railton, South Africa

"Being a father is something that has changed my life over and over and continues to change it to this day. When my daughter was born, I can't describe what went through me. That moment, the world I knew was gone. I was now living in a new world, where my only thoughts were of her. I saw things and possibilities where I had never seen them before. I know it sounds crazy, but that's what happened. I was lucky enough to have that happen again when I met Bonnie. She had two children from a previous relationship but I fell in love with them. They became my children. I wanted to keep them safe and help them excel. Never before and I experienced that with any other person or people. Those two will always be my kids even though biology had nothing to do with it. And I have been given that gift one final time. My son that has been around now for 10 years. It hit me that day just as it did but on the day my daughter was born. Being a father is something I wouldn't trade for anything on this planet, and any man that gets the opportunity to become one, I say buckle up. The ride you're about to take is wild, but there is no better feeling you'll have than while you're on it."

- Robert Bellamy, Canada

"When you become a dad, your life is kind of changing forever. Before my son's birth, I politely smiled and nodded as well-meaning people kept trying to prepare me for fatherhood by telling me the very often heard phrases like: "Say goodbye to your social life or get plenty of sleep now, because soon you'll be wishing you could." Sure, there is some truth in their advice, but there's also a bright side to the social and psychological changes you go through after becoming a dad. Certainly you are evolving, because one chapter of your life's path finishes and starts new one when your child is born. Another experience for you and continuity of the life. Definitely your perspective about the life is changing by the same moment when your child is getting born. Your senses are more opening, you become more aware of the things around you and in the world not just because you have a child but it is a common thing and it is connected with many other things in the nature. Becoming a father is not just having kid and just because of that you have to work harder to make more money and be serious! This is something more than that! It is a creation of new life which you have to nurture and grow with love and carefulness. You are creating another human being who will become in new grown person one day with his/her own life but carrying your roots and the roots of your predecessors. And this is not just continuity of the circle of life, but also you become wiser person and new horizons show up on our path!"

- Jorde Angelovic, Macedonia

"Becoming a father is a significant life changing event. As many know me for my youthful spirit and my borderline reckless acts of harmless fun, fatherhood meant that it was time to grow up and look at life from a more serious perspective.

This new perspective didn't happen overnight for me, if fact it evolved overtime and is still slowly evolving. Caring for my kids and their beautiful mother and partner for life is my absolute number one priority in life. My advice to new fathers out there is to make your kids and family your number one priority, the sooner the better. Teach them right from wrong and shield them from harm. Becoming a father is extremely rewarding giving me personally a huge feeling of success and happiness. No doubt there will be those great moments and challenging times, both beautiful and infuriating and sometimes both together!"

- Cliff Roebuck, Canada

"I am a blessed dad!

Together, my wife Dianne and I raised our 3 children. It was when I saw them for the first time that I realized that they were a gift from God. My perspective on life changed because suddenly there were 3 little ones counting on their dad to provide guidance, insights into life, love and yes, even proper discipline so that they would one day grow up, have a family of their own and positively pour into the lives of those they love. The love I have for my children pales in significance when compared to how much God the Father loves me and my family. After all, I was on His mind when He died on the cross and as a dad, I tried to instill that into the hearts of my children. One of my favourite verses is found in Proverbs 3: 5,6. "Trust in the Lord with all thy heart. Lean not on your own understanding. In all ways, acknowledge Him and He will guide and direct thy paths". Pictured here moments before I gave my beautiful daughter Brooke away in marriage.

- Rick Nicholls, Canada

"Being a dad didn't really come with a set of instructions so I had to bring up my inner child, the one that we all have deep in our hearts. I think the key is to always listen to your heart and never stop looking for those answers well hidden back in our childhood."

\- Elvis Ciurariu, Romania

"Before my daughter Evelynn arrived, I was living in my home country England, I was in a relationship with her Canadian mother to be, Tanya. My relationship with Evelynn's mother was not working out, I decided to move to Canada when Evelynn was one year old, so that I could be around for Evelynn on a regular basis. In short, I left my family and friends to be in my daughter's life, and I started a new life in Chatham, Ontario, a small town. I find that in my 30's, a lot of my parents upbringing, is reflected in the way I treat my daughter, but with a twist. Being a father has made me realise how much I love my daughter, and I now look at other children and feel a similar love and appreciation. I find it hard to find the fine lines between being a father, and simply growing up from twenties and into my thirties. I believe that being a father has helped to put me more in touch with my heart."

- Mark Requena, Canada

"Being a parent has changed me in a way that i never thought was possible. It is a journey that started on October 14, 1999 at 7:47pm. It has the ultimate highs and the lowest lows. A high is when I walk through the door after a hard day's work and your children run to you with their arms open wide and saying "daddy, daddy, I love you" Wow, what a feeling. Another high is also being there for their sporting events, when they lose and when they win, just being there for them is a victory for me. Also for their schooling events and awards, when your child receives an award, wow, I feel so proud on their accomplishments and achievements with goals behind them, to reach for the sky. What a feeling to be a part of that. And there are lows, when they get a little older and they say they hurt themselves somehow, just to be there to say it will be okay. When they cry, you wish you could take the pain for them, but I do know that someday will come, when I have to give my daughter to a man that I hope will and can, love her as much as I have throughout the years. Also my son, that he is a God fearing man like no other and for him to know how to treat a women respectfully as we have raised him too. I love these kids so much. A love that can only be shared by their dad and children. I guess your question to me would be love? It's not just us anymore, it's a family of four, and God. Just winging it. Don't worry you'll be fine. Don't forget, love and being a big part of your child's life, is the ultimate gift. Put your trust in God, he will never leave you or forsake you. God bless."

- Korey Payne, Canada

"Jimmy says fatherhood brings a lot more responsibilities, but along with that, comes an unbelievable amount of unconditional love! Your child becomes an extension of you and what having a child does is bring a kind of love to your heart that you have never had!"

- Melanie Fouch Hodge, USA

"How did becoming a father change me? The answer didn't come as easy as I thought it would. Of course there are the many clichés and they are all true; (becoming a father changes everything; it enriches your life in ways you can't imagine and it's the best job in the world etc.) but I wanted to dig a little deeper instead of giving a cookie cutter answer.

For me, I think the biggest change children have made in my life is that I am always asking myself "What impact / How will this affect my kids?" whenever I am about to say; do or decide anything. It is amazing how many times I stop and ask myself these questions on a daily basis. I lived the single life well into my late thirties and I was very egocentric, selfish and impulsive. Now; I really do think of my kids first before I act. I think it has made me a better; more responsible and healthier person. I want to be there for my kids as much as humanly possible; today, tomorrow and well into the future and this is the driving motivation in my thought process daily. Before I was the center of the universe; now I am a life support system for my children. There honestly really isn't much I wouldn't do for my kids if they asked. That is a crazy power I have willingly given to two other human beings over my life.

On the flip side; having kids is like having a giant exposed Achilles heel. When I was single I used to travel the darkest corners of the world and I felt untouchable and invulnerable. Now I feel like I am constantly on red alert when I walk out the front door. It is a

strange and uncomfortable shift for me. Having children has made me more accepting of my own death. I think knowing that I will be survived by my two daughters will make my last moments more peaceful; especially if they are close by me when the time comes. On my youngest daughter's birthday I posted a small passage that elaborates on this thought; I was very surprised about how many other people were moved and affected by this simple little passage. This is what I wrote: "Five years ago you came into my life; a bright dynamic force. You have truly been my little angel; making my feet lighter as I walk every single day."

That said - if I am being honest - I want to live to see my youngest daughter's 50th birthday party. Anything less than that I think I will feel cheated. If I have that honour I think I can leave this life peacefully and complete.

Lastly I want to share a story that happened a few years ago because I think it will tie all of these thoughts together nicely. For many years I had re-occurring nightmares that I'm on a commercial airline flight and something goes wrong, the dream inevitably ends in a crash. Most nights I would wake up panicked and sweaty after the crash. After having kids; the airplane crash nightmares came with the same frequency but where less stressful. In some dreams I would remember I have kids and it comforted me as the plane went down. Some dreams I would close my eyes, picture them and hear "Bittersweet Symphony" by The Verve playing in my head.

Fast forward a few years; I am taking my family on a cruise vacation and we have to take a plane to Miami Florida where the ship is in port. I am sitting with my youngest and my wife is sitting across from us with the oldest. Everything went smoothly and we were gear down seconds away from the rear wheels touching

down. The plane all of the sudden goes full thrust and sharply banks almost eighty degrees up and to the right and heads out towards the ocean; like the pilot is trying to avoid any population. The plane is dead quiet and my stomach is in my throat. I look over to my wife and our eyes met. In that moment we both knew without saying a word that our family was about to die. I then looked down to our daughters. Both seemed oblivious to what was really going on. My youngest was already holding my hand on the descent and she maintained her delicate grip. I wasn't thinking about faith. I wasn't thinking about religion. I didn't hear "Bittersweet Symphony" playing in my head. All I could think about was how innocent and precious my youngest looked; how trusting and safe she felt sitting there holding my hand like nothing was wrong. The airplane banked some more, straightened up and began to climb. It was only after we reached a safe altitude that the pilot came on and informed us that another plane had crossed our runway and he had to take emergency manoeuvres to avoid a collision. It was the most painful five minutes of my life and I wish that experience on no one; but we really appreciated and treasured every minute of that cruise with our children. I now have to travel on different flights from my youngest daughter and I still get anxiety when I replay the incident in my mind. And then I remember the clichés... and they are all true."

- Derek Herd, Canada

I hope that you got to read them all and to see that your purpose in this world is the most beautiful thing that God could give you: the opportunity to feel and act like Him, to understand Him and to grow closer to Him every day of your life... just by being a father.

Who Is Florin Marksteiner?

I THOUGHT THAT YOU MIGHT WANT TO KNOW ME.

Now, before you can find out official stuff about me, let me tell you what's close to my heart: I love everything that God put on this world, I am the type of person that if a butterfly goes by I stop and admire, I love the sun, the wind, the tripping of the birds, the smells that the wind brings from the fields and gardens, I take in every second and every step, I love to make use of the best gift that God gave me: **Life**. Because my roots are in Romania, a part of my heart will always be there and right not is hurting because of the dreadful situation that some people are living over there so I decided that a part of this book proceeds will go to help the poor people that you'll see in the pictures below. There is a good man doing great work with those poor souls there, but it's not enough. He needs our help. The link below is a simple campaign that I started so I can help somehow and maybe involve you too. **Even $1 is helping enormously.** The campaign is to build houses and can you believe that they can build a little house there with only **$5,000**? They do and I hope I can send them the first money for a house pretty soon. Please visit the link, like and share, and if you feel you can help, donate a little money.

http://bit.ly/5000house

Meet Pastor Paul Marica:

a father and a grandpa with a big heart for those that are forgotten by the "civilized society" and even by their families, a man that took God's word and applied it to his life and to those who surround him. Now I hope that, through this book and this message more help will be on the way and more people will be able to smile again because of a roof over their heads, food and clothes and some little gifts for the little ones.

Here are some pictures with some of the people God guided him to help and to bring some bright moments to their lives.

I need to tell you that I was so moved by this gentleman's story and of what he's doing there, that I needed to get involved the support him. I am really glad that I have a way to do it and if you're readying this right now even you contributed because, as I said, money from this book are going their way. But if you have a look at this pictures and you feel like you can do more, get involve, share with your friends and, once again, every little help, helps...

With no food and shelter, still willing to share a smile
when someone visits.

Homes are crumbling under the times. No one left to help.
Inside: forgotten elders.

144

Elders forgotten by the world and families living with no shelter or food, having no money, but having God in their hearts.

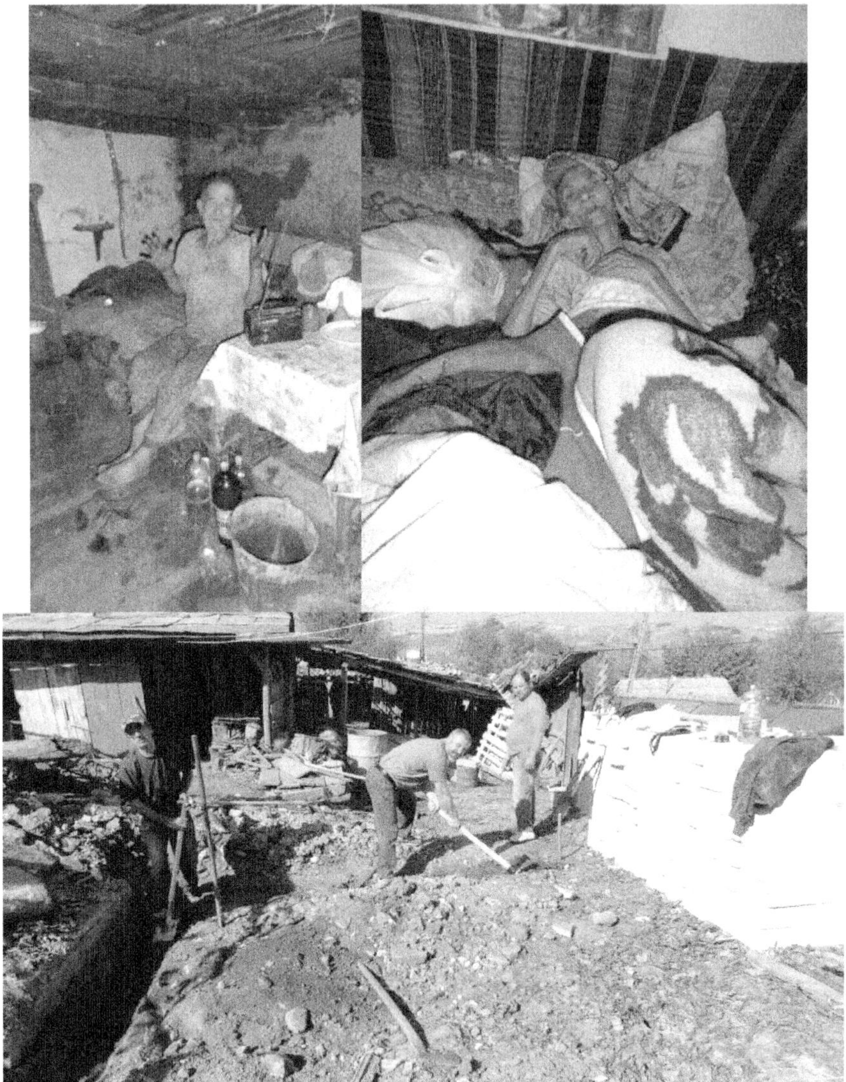

This is a pastor in action.
Digging and laying foundation for a small $5,000 home.
They came up with the simple "blueprint" so
they can bring shelter to as many needy people
as they can help.

Involved in every step, hoping that will be able to scale and build more.

Happy moments when the red roof is put in place. A sign that soon someone will be able to have shelter, a stove and a decent life.

Not just food for the stomachs,
but for the heart and soul too
with the Grace of God.

A t-shirt is more than a Christmas gift to a child:
it's a warm, clean, good lucking blessing.

Gathering full communities to praise God: priceless.

Sharing a slice of watermelon with all the kids is priceless.

Seeing the smiles brighten up their little sad faces: priceless.

Families with no money, no possibilities and no basic hygienic supplies,
raising children and loving them, giving them as much as they can
under God's mercy.

This is what you can make them look and feel like
if you decide to help a little bit.

Now... I can talk a little bit about myself... And I do it just because I want to you know me better. I hope that by now you feel you do.

"Originally from Romania and growing up under tough conditions in communism, Florin can say that he lived on both sides of the wall. After the Revolution in 1989 he, and the entire Romanian people, had to adapt to capitalism and find a career. Because of his personality, Florin was attracted by the entertainment industry and in particular by acting and film making. Today, after 20 years in the industry, Florin is continuing his career on the other side of the planet, on the North American continent, precisely in Canada and extended his writing skills from film scripts and commercial copy-writing to becoming a publish author."

1. **Director/Actor**
   http://www.imdb.com/name/nm4701284
   http://bit.ly/haydarinterview

2. **Local news about me**
   http://www.chathamdailynews.ca/2013/09/15/ten-florin-marksteiner

3. **I have my own film TV production company**
   http://www.productionmark.ca

4. **Film producer**
   Press:
   http://www.lfpress.com/2013/10/20/documenting-tecumsehs-last-days
   Here's some trailers:
   Like A Hero Going Home
   https://www.youtube.com/watch?v=imabCLgt_go
   Daughter of the King - Feature Film
   http://bit.ly/dotktrailer

Elvis: The Legend Continues - Documentary
http://bit.ly/elvisdoctrailer
The Cultured Criminal - Historic Film
http://bit.ly/theculturedcriminaltrailer

5. **Festival Director Christian Life International Film Festival**
http://www.cliffest.com
Press:
http://www.ckreview.ca/2013/09/cliff-film-festival-brings-people-to-chatham-kent/
http://www.chathamdailynews.ca/2013/09/22/great-potential-for-christian-film-festival

6. **I own an independent online radio station - Radio CK**
http://www.radiock.ca
http://www.facebook.com/radiockca
Press:
http://www.chathamvoice.com/2015/04/02/radio-ck-is-on-the-air/

7. **Public Speaker**
To book me to inspire and motivate:
http://bit.ly/bookflorin

Lately I co-found an actors and filmmakers group that produces ice breakers to help congregations to bring Jesus in the discussion easier:

We want to move the masses, which means, we want to touch them with our films and move them towards Jesus and God, towards Salvation.

http://www.12disciples.ca

Next you'll see how you can get your congregation involved in the great harvest with 12 Disciples.

12 Disciples

MOVING THE MASSES

Did you ever think that we are becoming disciples of our parents by continuing and passing on their traditions, their habits, their lessons of life and their love? Yes, we do the same thing that the disciples did for Jesus... at a smaller scale, but we do it and it's embedded in us.

The reason why I ask you this question was to show you how simple it is to be a disciple once you know what you want to pass onto others. There is a group of Christian Filmmakers that we started , "12 Disciples" and we have one single purpose: to spread the Gospel and the word about Jesus with film. Check the website and if you like what we do, share with your friends and most importantly with your congregation to see how your group can get involved in the program and enjoy all the benefits that come with it.

Website: http://www.12disciples.ca
Facebook: http://www.facebook.com/12disciplesca
Twitter: http://www.twitter.com/12disciplesca

Click or scan to watch some powerful videos.

See what the group does

Check the Facebook Page

Watch Feature Film Trailer

Watch a powerful message

Watch "J..."

[15 minutes]

I need to share this with you:

Being a filmmaker and loving good films with powerful messages I would like to share with you a helpful website that can provide you with that: ChristianFilmDatabase.com

Here's what the founders tell you about the CFDb story:

Roger and Annelie Rudlaff are avid Christian film lovers who desire to get the word out about Christian films. Over the years we found out that most people think the only Christian films out there are titles such as Moses, Joseph and Jesus of Nazareth. While those films are great, there is so much more out there and Roger wondered how are people going to know.

So began... The Wayhouse Christian Film Library – a free service to the community where people could come and check out Christian movies/documentaries/cartoons and return them for more. It started off slowly and as we moved to different locations the greatest success was in Roanoke, VA where we even made the front page of the

newspaper. It was successful in getting the word out locally, although not successful financially, for obvious reasons.

An unexpected family crisis arose causing us to close up shop and move again – no more Wayhouse but another development came from this... CFDb. It started very slowly in 2008 and in 2011 we formed an LLC company, (Christianfilmdatabase.com, LLC), and began to try and figure out ways so we could spend more time on the database because every film and everything done with the database is all done by Roger or Annelie, except for web issues that come up, including getting the search to work better, which thanks to Bryce, it now works wonderfully!

Scan and enjoy!

A little hope note

I do hope that you reached to this page and you did enjoy the book. As I said, it came from a moment of inspiration and, in the creation process, I just ridden the wave that brought me to this finished product. I know it's not perfect and I know I might not be right in everything I say in here, but I hope that I pulled wide open the curtains of the dark room you're in right now and that the sunlight is shining warmly on your face producing a big wide smile putting you in another stance with more hope and more understanding in what a great position you are and how you are, above any earthly adversity, understanding Our Father, God.

Florin

Printed in Great Britain
by Amazon

60652772R00102